The Practice of Sacred Music

The Practice of Sacred Music

Chairman, Department of Music
Concordia Teachers College
River Forest, Illinois

CONCORDIA PUBLISHING HOUSE — Saint Louis, Missouri

LIBRARY OF CONGRESS CATALOG NUMBER 55-7441

MANUFACTURED IN THE UNITED STATES OF AMERICA

To My Parents

Of the Father's love begotten
Ere the worlds began to be,
He is Alpha and Omega,
He the Source, the Ending He,
Of the things that are, that have been,
And that future years shall see
Evermore and evermore.

Oh, that birth forever blessed
When the Virgin, full of grace
By the Holy Ghost conceiving,
Bare the Savior of our race,
And the Babe, the world's Redeemer,
First revealed His sacred face
Evermore and evermore.

O ye heights of heaven, adore Him;
Angel hosts, His praises sing;
Powers, dominions, bow before Him
And extol our God and King.
Let no tongue on earth be silent,
Every voice in concert ring
Evermore and evermore.

Corde natus ex Parentis
AURELIUS PRUDENTIUS, † 413

Foreword

REPEATEDLY the music editors of Concordia Publishing House have been requested to make available a publication which might serve as a guide to pastors, choirmasters, organists, and others who concern themselves with the practice of Christian church music. He who undertakes to prepare a publication of this kind must have a wide acquaintance with the field of church music, a sympathetic approach to the problems of the Church and her worship, an understanding of basic liturgical principles and procedures, and a successful experience as a choirmaster, organist, teacher, and leader. The editorial committee was unanimously of the opinion that Prof. Carl Halter, Mus. M., was eminently qualified to prepare such a work and encouraged him to proceed with the preparation of the present volume, to which the author gave the simple but pertinent title THE PRACTICE OF SACRED MUSIC.

The very fact that numerous requests were received for the publication of a manual of this kind indicates not only that many feel they need help and direction, but also that those who are responsible directly as well as indirectly for the practice of church music desire to heed the Scriptural injunction that they do their work decently and in order (1 Cor. 14:40). In recent years rapid forward strides have been made to improve the musical expression in Christian worship. It is our belief that Professor Halter's thought-provoking and instructive manual will be a real contribution. It will serve to raise the standard of musical performance in the services of worship conducted in the Christian churches of our time. Thus the name of God will be used in a manner that will redound to the glory of Him whom Christian people worship and adore as their Creator, Redeemer, and Sanctifier.

WALTER E. BUSZIN

Concordia Seminary
Saint Louis, Missouri

Preface

THE music of the Church is never the private preserve of clergy and musicians. If music is to serve as an instrument of worship, it must be meaningful for all. The present volume is intended not only for those who lead in worship, but also for lay persons who participate in the music of the Church and who are alive to the importance of music in the life of the Church. This volume strives to establish the fundamental principles upon which a significant musical life may be based, and to suggest in a general way how these principles may be put into practice.

It is offered with the conviction that music and musical practices are not of minor concern in the life of the Church; that there is reciprocal action between music and faith; that the music which we use in worship is so closely allied with the center and heart of Christian faith and life that it must never be ignored in favor of things which appear more "practical"; that here, too, the things of the spirit are more powerful and more important than the things of the flesh.

It is the author's hope that in this volume the whole body of the Church may find some one thing, if it is only that, which will help it to praise God more completely and spread His name more widely.

CARL HALTER

River Forest, Illinois
Fourth Sunday in Advent, 1953

Acknowledgments

I wish to express my indebtedness to many persons who during the course of the past years have enriched my experiences by sharing with me their own. In particular, I should like to thank the following: Mr. Edward Klammer of the Music Department of Concordia Publishing House for asking me to write the book and for being patient in the process; the members of the Music Committee of Concordia Publishing House for careful reading of the manuscript and for valuable suggestions; and my colleague, Mr. Paul Bunjes, for much of the material in chapter 10.

Contents

CHAPTER 1

Christian Worship

THE subject of the worship of God is a vast and fascinating one. The mind of man is inescapably attracted to the problems of infinity and eternity and their Source and Being. The longing for the infinite and eternal is characteristic of all religions, whether natural or revealed. Also the heathen seeks to attune his life to the demands of powers greater than himself, and he inevitably develops certain techniques and forms to accomplish his end. In this sense, we may say that all men worship. In the present discussion, however, we shall pass by all the ramifications of an anthropological examination of worship and consider only the worship of the Triune God, the God of Christianity.

The first problem in Christian worship is that of volition. While it is true that all men wish to worship, it is also true that all men wish to construct their own gods. Man does not wish to worship the God of the Bible. Self-created gods can be appeased by self; but the God of the Bible can be appeased only by Himself. This fact requires of man an act of self-renunciation which no man has ever been willing to perform, unless enabled to do so by an act of God. "The carnal mind is enmity against God." Luther put it this way: "I believe that I cannot by my own reason or strength believe in Jesus Christ, my Lord, or *come to Him,* but the Holy Ghost has called me by the Gospel, enlightened me with His gifts, sanctified, and kept me in the true faith."

The desire of a *Christian* to worship, then, is not a product of his own will, but of God's. It is important for the conduct of worship that this point be fully appreciated. There is no merit earned by the act of worship. Worship itself is an evidence of God's grace, a gift from Him for us to savor and enjoy.

The second problem is that of form or method. In all the periods of the Church's life the problem of the manner of the approach to God has brought forth much concern and many words. This concern has been as evident, though not in the same way, among nonliturgical churches as among liturgical. Puritan austerity is as much a result of a concern with the approach to God as are votive lights and the

St. Matthew Passion. Among Christians the question in debate has never been: "Shall God be approached?" but rather: "How shall God be approached?"

Worship has been experienced in many ways, and all these ways can be and are useful in illuminating the subject. The very multiplicity of experiences reveals the essential subjectivity of worship. Not all men can and do worship God in the same manner. Forms of worship are affected by such variable factors as time, place, language, and theological emphasis. Because of the great variety of experiences possible, worship is not subject to pat definition, or close and exact analysis. Worship is a growing, emerging force, not an accomplished and codified method safely embalmed in rules. Finally, it cannot be defined; it can only be experienced and, perhaps, described. If, however, we seek to penetrate to the essence of true worship, we shall probably arrive at some synthesis such as this, from whichever divergent viewpoint we may begin: *Worship is joyful concern with God through Christ.*

The subject of Christian worship is God. Perhaps this point of view becomes clearest by antithesis. The end of worship is not man. It is not liturgy, or music, or liturgical accessories, but God and only God. It must be emphasized here that there is one prime condition which God Himself has set for all worship: We can approach God only through the Mediator, whom He Himself appointed — Jesus, the Christ. It is only because Christ died and paid the price of reunion that man can hope to be once more at one with his Maker, Redeemer, and Sanctifier. In the sense in which we here use the term, there is no worship where Christ is ignored or denied.

Worship is concern, arising out of faith and love of God. It is not a passive viewing, or even only adoration. It is an active concern, which asks God's will as revealed in His Word, studies it, and seeks to respond to it.

And worship is joy. The study of God can end only in love and joy. There is no joy in man's experience which can equal the meeting and appreciation of the Divinity. "I was glad when they said unto me, Let us go into the house of the Lord" is a common experience of the heart versed in worship. It is the expectant joy of the bridegroom and the bride. It is the fulfilled joy of the Prodigal Son come home. It is these and more, as God is more.

Worship is an art rather than a science. There is, of course, an element of science in any art, but the art suffers when it becomes overbalanced by the scientific aspect. A coldly scientific and calculating

2

approach to worship is impossible without the negation of worship. The worshiper cannot predetermine the desired gains to be achieved, and then calculate his petitions and devotions to secure them. Worship is not a problem in engineering.

Worship is an art because it is a means of uniting two intangibles: God and the human heart. In what state these two may be, only God and the human heart can know at any given moment. The intuitive and happy search of each for the other is the wonder, the excitement, and the reward of true worship.

From the standpoint of the Christian who urgently loves God, the reward of worshiping God is the very fact of worship. This is true of all situations where love is the dominant impulse, because love, among other things, is forgetfulness of self. For the loving Christian, then, it is enough that God permits and encourages him to worship. He asks no blessing other than to be in the company of God. But God in His mercy showers upon the Christian worshiper all the eternal and temporal blessings which He has promised in His Word. These blessings are, as it were, a bonus, pressed into the already overflowing cup of the Christian. "Seek ye first the kingdom of God and His righteousness, and all these things shall be added unto you."

Private Worship

When worship is carried on by the individual Christian alone with his God, the element of art in worship can be raised to its highest level of perfection, for only in this relationship can the art of artlessness be enjoyed. Here there is no prescription of subject matter or form. The praise and enjoyment of God can be carried on without thought of adhering to, or measuring up to, standards set in part by other human beings. The relationship can be childlike and artless.

Private worship has also the advantage that it provides freedom from distractions. A number of necessary mechanical appurtenances, beginning with the building itself and its decoration, may serve to distract a worshiper in public worship. Perhaps one of the most distracting features in public worship is the presence of other personalities, notably the liturgist and musicians, but including also all the other worshipers. In private one can be alone with God. Perhaps the chief value of private worship lies in the fact that it enables the individual to bring his own particular problems, fears, needs, and gratitude to God. At best, public worship affords the opportunity to do this only in a nonspecific way.

3

Individual worship has, however, the weaknesses of all individualism. It is confined to the experience of one person and is therefore restricted in scope and likely to become self-centered. It is also likely to degenerate into mere sentimentalism or purposeless frenzy because it is so completely free and unchecked.

In spite of these defects, however, the personal piety which expresses itself in quiet, lonely devotions composed of the reading of Scripture, prayers, and hymns is an art which should be more cultivated among us.

Public or Corporate Worship

Corporate worship — worship by a congregation of believers — has other excellencies and other problems. When the congregation worships, agreed forms must be used so that all may be done decently and in order. This means that a compromise must be effected with regard to liturgy, music, and ceremonial, since not all who worship together will agree with respect to the materials and methods employed. The danger here is not so much in the fact that a compromise needs to be made as it is in the fact that the function of compromising tends to replace the function of worship. Thus choirs and organists worry not so much about the fitness of their work for the praise of God and the edification of man as about the reception of their work by the congregation or about the historical and musical correctness of their selection and performance.

But corporate worship secures important values to the believer. There is a sense of confidence experienced in the use of familiar and beloved liturgical forms, hymns, and music. The possibilities in worship are enlarged by the use of ideas and modes of expression all of which would not occur to any one individual. And then there is present that heightened sense of awareness which comes only when people willingly co-operate in any activity. The average worshiper sings with more enthusiasm and with less self-consciousness when he can sing with the whole community of believers.

Tradition in Worship

One other advantage of corporate worship brings us to a brief discussion of the role of tradition in worship. The advantage is that most of the elements used in any service are of other than contemporary origin. When we attend an average service, we sing hymns and chants and use responses and listen to prayers which have been used by generations and centuries of the saints back to the Apostolic era and beyond. This sense of unity with all the believers in Christ, regardless of time, is one of the chief fruits of corporate worship. God is contemporary because He meets our needs today; but God is much more than merely contemporary. "Before Abraham was, I am."

Another value to be secured by the use of tradition is to be found in the rich storehouse of faith and beauty which the saints of other days have created out of their love of God. How uncomprehending it would be to ignore the Apostles' Creed, or "A Mighty Fortress," or the Cathedral of Chartres! How wasteful and contemptuous of God's gifts!

And yet tradition can become a danger to the Church. It becomes a danger when it is so far from the experience of the worshiper that it becomes a spiritless form, or when it is chosen and used not primarily for its value for the souls who use it, but rather primarily for its artistic and historic value. It is dangerous when it ceases to give Christian joy by uniting souls with God.

It is just at this point that the difficulties of those who lead in public worship center. The liturgist and the musician can be expected to know the traditions of Christian worship and to be able to use them. More to the point, however, they must know how to discover and reveal their relevance to the souls now worshiping. Some traditions in worship are so far removed from the experience and culture of contemporary Christians that it becomes necessary for them to learn an entire foreign culture before they can participate. In such situations it would seem the part of charity and wisdom to forego the ancient usage, no matter how beautiful, in favor of a form which has more immediacy for the worshiper.

Beyond this, however, it must be noted that worship should be, and, in its highest practice is, creative. The Church of today need not assume that all the necessary or possible ways of worshiping God have been explored. Worship should be a spiritual adventure also for the Christians of our own day. Too great an emphasis upon tradition and historical correctness inevitably serves to stultify the creative urge in man. If the Church of today becomes interested liturgically only in resurrecting the usages of the past, no matter how beautiful, it will pass nothing to its sons except that which it has exhumed and transcribed. This would be a valuable legacy in itself, but it would not be all that is possible nor all that is desirable. It would not reflect the vital spiritual experiences of an entire era of believers.

5

Conclusion

Worship is a joyful concern with God through Christ. It is imperative that the church musician realize the meaning and implications of this general description, for without an understanding of the worship which he is to aid, he can destroy it. Equipped with an understanding of the great adventure of worship, he can contribute mightily to the strengthening of the Body of Christ.

He can give his people an awareness of the transcendent importance of worship. It has been well said that the whole purpose of man's life is "to glorify God and to enjoy Him forever." (Westminster Catechism.) In a day when the Church is secularized, he can help turn it to things spiritual. In a day when the Church, misguided, thinks its function is political, or economic, or social, he can help direct it once again to the heart of God and the soul of man. In a day when the Church is choked with societies and their activities, he can help to provide an arena for the gracious God and the seeking soul.

CHAPTER 2

Music in Worship

It is possible, of course, to worship without music. Any spoken or unspoken prayer or thought of God done in love of God is worship. But it is nonetheless a significant fact that the experience of the Church in all ages has been that when the heart is filled and warm toward God, music is heard. This was true of David as well as of the lonely Negro slave, and is true of every mother singing a prayer for her child. It is natural for the human spirit to resort to music when worshiping because worship enlists the deepest and strongest emotions — those emotions which go beyond words and demand greater expression.

We find, also, that both the Old and the New Testament are replete with injunctions for the use of music in the praise of God. The Book of Psalms, the hymnbook of the Old Testament Church, repeats the injunction "Sing unto the Lord" many times. The public worship of the Old Testament Church made extensive use of music and required the services of a large number of highly organized professional musicians. The New Testament confirms and adopts the musical practices of the Old Testament Church. The New Testament Church continued the musical usages of the synagog and the Temple, with only such additions and changes as were necessitated by the acceptance of Jesus as the Christ.

It is beyond the scope of this book to explore the development and use of music in the Church from that time to this. It is, however, important to note that virtually until the death of Bach (1750) the main stream of the development of music was in the Church. Popular music was, of course, always in existence. But serious composers almost unanimously received their inspiration from, and dedicated their works to, the Church.

Such a close and consistent association between religion and music rooted in God's will and practiced through the centuries by all of His saints is no mere haphazard or accidental relation. Music occupies a peculiarly high and important place in the practice of the Christian religion.

7

The chief, and perhaps only, difference between the music of the Church and secular music is a difference in function. Where secular music is free to address itself to any of man's emotions, the music of the Church is restricted to serving the Word of God, its presentation to man, and man's response to the Word. Church music is never an end in itself; nor is its function to entertain.

A quotation at this point from Paul Henry Lang's book, *Music in Western Civilization,* will serve to illustrate how from the time of the earliest Church Fathers sacred music was separated from the popular song of the people by a simple test of function: "Music could be considered by the Church only if it served the purposes of the Church, and therefore the subject and aim of Christian cult music was and remained the *gloria Dei* and the *aedificatio hominum,* the glorification of God and the edification of man." [1] This simple principle was in common acceptance all through the history of the Christian Church and is characteristic of the best church music practices of our own day. Wherever it is forgotten, church music is in decline.

We may distinguish a number of functions which music performs in carrying out its service to God and man in the Church. At the very lowest level it serves a purely practical purpose in aiding the congregation to proceed with greater unanimity through the liturgy or form used in the service. It is easier to have a congregation sing a hymn than it is to have the same group of people read in chorus a prose or even poetic selection. The rhythm of the music is easily apprehended and serves to unite all the individuals worshiping. So also the almost constant flow of music during the liturgical portions of the service tends to knit the service together and to provide continuity.

Secondly, we must recognize a didactic purpose in the use of music by the Church. The educational value of music in connection with words has been one of the main reasons for the creation and use of hymns by the Church. In the second century of the Christian era there arose among the Greek Christians a sect called the Gnostics, which used hymns to inculcate a "practical" Christianity. Unfortunately, false doctrines also slipped into their hymns. Faced with the great popularity of these heretical hymns, the Church itself was stimulated to the production of hymns which were orthodox. Thus began the history of Greek hymnody, a history which produced, among many other fruits, the beautiful hymn of Synesius of Cyrene (died c. 414), "Lord Jesus, Think on Me."

[1] Paul Henry Lang, *Music in Western Civilization* (New York: W. W. Norton & Co., Inc., 1941), p. 41.

Latin hymnody had a similar beginning. In the early fourth century the Arians followed the example of the Greek Gnostics and produced hymns to popularize their approach to Christianity. Again the orthodox Church was forced to react, and thus began the glorious history of Latin hymnody, which produced Hilary, Ambrose, and Bernard of Clairvaux, and the great Latin hymns which we still use or which fertilized the German renaissance under Luther.

Martin Luther is notable among great leaders of the Church also for his high estimate of the art of music and his very real proficiency in it. His interest in hymnody, however, was strongly influenced by the purely practical consideration of its didactic value. He reasoned that if he could lead the people to sing the truths of God's Word, in an easily remembered form, that both the understanding and retention of these truths would be greatly aided. In a letter to Spalatinus in 1523 Luther wrote: "Following the example of the Prophets and Church Fathers, I intend to supply German psalms or religious songs, so that the Word of God may live among the people also in musical form."[2] In his commentary on 2 Sam. 23:1 Luther states in part: "Music and notes, the creation and gift of God, are aids to spiritual understanding, especially when sung earnestly by a congregation."[3]

It is not surprising, therefore, that one of the chief by-products of the Reformation was a flowering of music culminating in the great works of Bach, and all based ultimately upon texts and tunes of the chorales which Luther helped to create and which he used for the purpose of instruction.

This point probably needs no further emphasis. The didactic value of hymns is experienced by all who have learned fine Christian hymns in their youth and who recall their words and music when they are old, thereby strengthening their faith in the truths there expressed.

These first two functions of music in the Church, when compared with other and higher values, are somewhat mechanical functions. Music is valued as a device for securing a certain mechanical unanimity in public worship and as a method for inculcating the truths of God's Word. But music in the Church is much more than a device. When music is looked upon by musicians, clergy, or people merely as a handy tool to be called upon when needed for some purely practical reason, the chief functions of music are denied it. Music's chief value for worship lies in

---

[2] Martin Luther, Sämmtliche Schriften, herausgegeben von Dr. J. G. Walch. Neue revidierte Stereotypausgabe, trans. Carl Halter and Margaret Hermes. (St. Louis: Concordia Publishing House, 1880.) Vol. XXIa: 582.

[3] St. L., III: 1888.

the realm of the spirit. Music has the power to move the soul of man for good or ill. When music is used in the praise of God and for the edification of man, it has the power to lift man's soul to greater appreciation of God and His love for man.

No one has ever valued music more highly in this respect than Luther. Quotation after quotation could be adduced in which Luther expressed his overwhelming appreciation of this function of music. Here, in part, is what Luther wrote in a preface to a publication of part songs in 1538:

> I am heartily eager that the divine and heavenly gift of music be praised before all men. But I am so overwhelmed by the multitude and greatness of its excellence and virtues that I can find neither beginning nor end, nor any adequate words to do it justice. . . .
>
> One ought also to speak of the use of such a great thing, but its use is so infinitely various that it is beyond the eloquence of the greatest orators. We will mention only this one point now: Experience testifies that, after the Word of God, only music deserves to be praised as the mistress and governess of the emotions of the human heart (regarding animals we say nothing here), by which emotions human beings are ruled and often torn asunder as if by their masters. A greater praise of music than this we cannot imagine. . . . It is out of consideration for this power of music that the Fathers and Prophets willed, and not in vain, that nothing be more closely bound up with the Word of God than music.[4]

Here let us be very clear on one important point: Music does not have the power to make God's love greater than it is. Music can add nothing to God, as neither can preaching or architecture or painting. But music does afford the most direct and effective avenue into the human heart of any of the arts, an avenue which God is pleased to use and encourage. It also has the power to lift the human heart to a sincere and healthy adoration of God and His works. It is in this realm of the spirit that music makes its great and unique contribution.

From time to time in the history of the Church there have been those who have sought to limit the area of music's function. They have said that music must be plain; that its sole function is to accompany, simply and dully, the congregation's singing; and a variety of other things all calculated to circumscribe and delimit the power of music

---

[4] St. L., XIV: 429, 430. It should be remembered that "church music" in Luther's time meant almost entirely "vocal music," i. e., music connected with words.

over the human soul. These voices are not entirely silent today. It is, however, in the best tradition of all church music, and certainly most markedly in the Lutheran tradition, that music ought to be developed to its greatest peak just here, where it is used in praise of God and for the uplifting of men's souls to Him. This is the reason for Bach's expending his tremendous artistic genius upon music for the Church. He would quite properly have considered it wrong for him to use less than his full powers on the music for divine service, saving the best for works dedicated to secular use.

Luther makes this point most emphatically. In his preface to the *Geistliches Gesangbuechlein* of 1524 Luther writes:

> I am not of the opinion, as are the heterodox, that for the sake of the Gospel all arts should be rejected and eliminated; rather, I feel strongly that all the arts, and particularly music, should be placed in the service of Him who has created and given them.[5]

In an uncompleted essay titled "Concerning Music," Luther wrote the following:

> I am not pleased with those who, like all the fanatics, despise music. Music is a gift of God, not of men. Music drives away the devil and makes people happy; in the presence of music one forgets all hate, unchastity, pride, and other vices. After theology I accord to music the highest place and the greatest honor.[6]

The church which neglects its music or assigns to it a purely pedestrian function, robs itself outrageously, and it flies in the face not only of the experience of the Church, but also of the will of God.

[5] St. L., X: 1424.

[6] St. L., XXII: 1541.

11

CHAPTER 3

Song in Worship

WE have noted that in Luther's day the music of the Church was almost exclusively vocal, i. e., music in accompaniment of words. Actually, this connotation has been true of the preponderance of music used in the entire history of the Church. In our day the use of the organ in the church has placed a greater emphasis upon instrumental music than had been customary earlier, but it is still true that most church music is still what we can in general term "vocal music."

Liturgical Chant

Historically, and in contemporary practice, we may distinguish four types or classes of church song. The earliest type has its origin in the Temple and synagog services of the Jews and has been transmitted to our own day virtually unchanged as to general characteristics. We may call this by a variety of names: liturgical song, chant, plainchant, Gregorian chant. It is the church song which the Early Christians inherited directly from their Jewish faith and which they used in their Christian worship, as they had previously used it in their synagog and Temple services. This Jewish-Christian chant, technically called cantillation, consisted of melodic formulas which were used in combination and extension in the reading of Scripture and the chanting of Psalms.

This basic church song was spread throughout Christendom by the dispersion of Christian Jews over the civilized world in the centuries following the time of Christ. It was subtly but not substantially altered by the effect upon it of local needs and characteristics. The next important step in its development was the work of Pope Gregory (590—604), who caused scholars to collect the various chants from all parts of the Church and to standardize them for use in the services of the Church. The so-called "Gregorian" chant which resulted from this activity was, therefore, a Jewish church song which had been enriched by six centuries of Christian activity among Jewish and Gentile peoples alike.

After Gregory the liturgical song continued to develop principally in its application to various additional liturgical texts, such as tropes and sequences. From the thirteenth and fourteenth centuries onward, however, plainchant ceased to be creative, and the development of church music took place in other forms.

The following brief example will serve to illustrate some of the characteristics of plainchant as it is still used in large sections of the Church today:[7]

Example 1

Cantate Domino

Can - tá - te   Dó - mi - no* cán - ti - cum

nó - vum.   Al - le - lú - ia.

The chief characteristics to be noted here are the following:

1. The text is in prose rhythm.

2. The music, particularly on reciting tones (see example 2) follows the rhythm and accents of the text. The music is in oratorical or declamatory style.

3. The music is melismatic, i. e., there are two or more notes to a syllable of text, except on reciting tones. (See example 2.)

4. There is a quietness and repose in the music, the result in great part of the limited rang of notes and the avoidance of dramatic contrasts and dynamic extremes.

5. The music is newly composed throughout; that is, it is not in the form of stanzas which are repeated, but rather in the form of one complete composition.

In most liturgical Churches today the chief use of plainchant is in connection with the chanting of the Introit and the Gradual. The

[7] Introit for Fourth Sunday after Easter. *Liber Usualis* (Tournai, Belgium: Desclee and Company, 1950), p. 826.

formulas or "tones" used in such chants are simplified recitation melodies such as the following:[8]

Example 2

Antiphon from Introit for the Feast of the Holy Trinity
Tone IV g

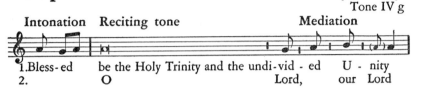

Intonation Reciting tone   Mediation

1.Bless-ed be the Holy Trinity and the undi-vid - ed U - nity
2.   O   Lord,   our Lord

Reciting tone   Termination

1. Let us give glory to Him because He hath shown His mercy to   us.
2. How excellent is Thy name in   all the earth.

These are quite easily mastered by the average church choir and are also quite readily accepted by the average contemporary congregation.

Congregational Song

The nature of liturgical chant precludes its use by large congregations of people and dictates its performance by a choir or soloist. Liturgical chant lacks a mechanical poetic and musical rhythm, and its proper rendition requires delicacy in nuance and unanimity in the cadence of words and music. For these reasons it is difficult, if not absolutely impossible, for large congregations of people without special training to participate effectively in the chant. This characteristic of the chant has caused those who wished to enlist the support of large numbers of musically untrained people to create music of a radically different style for their use. Hence the creation of hymnody.

Whatever the superficial differences may be among the various styles of congregational song created in the many epochs of Christian hymnody, there is at least one common denominator: hymns are made to be sung by the entire body of believers, trained or untrained. For this basic reason congregational song or hymnody has the following characteristics:

[8] Walter E. Buszin, *The Introits for the Church Year* (St. Louis: Concordia Publishing House, 1942), pp. 22, 23.

1. Both text and music have some sort of mechanical rhythm. There is a more or less regular and predictable recurrence of strong and weak beats — accent and release.
2. Text and music are lyrical in quality, rather than oratorical and declamatory.
3. The music is syllabic, having normally one note of music to one syllable of text.
4. There is a simplicity, forthrightness, and directness in both text and music which is calculated to meet the needs of masses of people.
5. The music is repeated stanza after stanza. (Strophic.)

These characteristics insure ease of performance, easy retention of both text and tune, and emotional participation on a level easily attainable by all worshipers. These are the outcomes sought by all those who have used chorales and hymns to supplement or replace liturgical chant. We have in Chapter II briefly noted the development of hymnody in the Greek, Latin, and German churches. A brief look at any standard hymnal in use today will reveal that a similar pattern obtains in English hymnody as well.

Choral Song

In both liturgical chant and hymnody the emphasis is placed primarily upon presentation of truth in as simple a manner as is consistent with the general style in each case. Stated negatively, the greatest emphasis is not placed upon artistic development either musically or textually. The Church has felt, however, that the greatest art of which man is capable ought to be placed in the Savior's service. For this reason, both liturgical chant and hymnody have produced a large body of choral song which is distinguished from its source by a greater artistic development of the materials inherent in the source. This, then, is music not intended for the congregation, but for the choir. Its purpose is to lift to a higher level the experiences of the average worshiper. To that end it uses texts and tunes familiar to the worshiper, but adorns them, develops them, and makes them meaningful on a higher, deeper plane.

MEDIEVAL AND RENAISSANCE MOTETS: (1300—1600)

As previously noted, the creative period of unison plainchant declined and ended during the thirteenth and fourteenth centuries. The desire to create did not die, however, but rather found a different outlet. It is not surprising to discover, therefore, that the period of the medieval motet begins in the thirteenth century. Musicians, very probably bored with the unchanged and unchanging repetition of the same unison chants, began to add a second melody to the chant, to be sung simultaneously with it, and also another text. The additional tune revealed the influence of popular and even secular music. It was usually in a mechanical rhythm and had a sweep and sway totally out of keeping with the grave, suave chant with which it was coupled. In fact, the chants were usually slowed down in tempo to such an extent that they were unrecognizable as chants, and the added voice attracted most of the interest and attention.

The texts also revealed popular trends. Sometimes the texts were amplifications of the liturgical text used with it, but often the additional text had nothing whatsoever to do with the liturgical text, and sometimes it was even a secular ballad in the vernacular of the people rather than in liturgical Latin.

Much more could well be said with regard to the medieval and Renaissance motets. Whatever the details of the development of these motets, however, the impulses which gave them birth were two: a desire to communicate more fully with the average believer, and a desire to employ the best powers of the art of music in the service of God. As time went on, the obviously objectionable features of the early motets were eliminated, more and more voices were added, and more and more artistic devices were invented until finally the glorious motets of Di Lasso and Palestrina were achieved. The works of these and many other composers of this period constitute a lasting legacy of enduring value to the Church.

CHORALE MOTET (1550—1750)

The musical aspect of the Lutheran Reformation was most fully and characteristically expressed in the chorale. The chorale is by definition the German religious congregational song which Luther created for reasons which have several times been noted in these pages. Luther himself, however, was not content that the simple chorale be the only musical expression of the faith. He was not willing, for instance, that the use of plainchant be eliminated from Lutheran services, and indeed, he went to some pains to indicate his views upon its fitting use. It is significant, however, that Luther versified and set to hymnlike tunes various parts of the liturgy which had previously been sung by the cantor or choir, so that now the entire congregation could participate. Examples of this are: "We All Believe in One True God," which is a versification of the Creed, and "Isaiah, Mighty Seer in Days of Old," which is an alternate setting of the Sanctus.

16

As a result of this liturgical use of the chorale, the chorale began to be used as the theme or *cantus firmus* of motets in the Lutheran Church, replacing the plainchant tune. The essential difference between the plainchant motet and the chorale motet is not in its use, for both were used liturgically. The difference lies in the basic material. In point of techniques used, the chorale motet is simply an extension of the Renaissance motet. In point of significance to the worshiper, however, there was a most important change: Henceforth the motet was built upon a tune and text which the worshiper had himself sung and whose text he had memorized. In brief, the art music of the Church had been brought home to the very doorstep of the average worshiper, and he could feel himself a part even of the monumental cantatas and Passions of Bach — all through the chorale.

THE ANTHEM

The anthem is historically an English motet. When the Reformation reached England, it brought about musical changes similar to those brought about in Germany. Among these the most significant were a development of English hymnody and the use of the vernacular as the liturgical language of the reformed Church. A change in language always causes a change in the music which is set to that language, and it is for this reason primarily that the anthem developed as a type distinct from the parent motet.

In point of function the anthem does not differ from the motet; both are intended to be used as part of the liturgy of worship. In point of style, however, a number of differences are apparent. The following brief list includes most of the distinguishing features:

1. The anthem is more syllabic than the motet.
2. The style is more harmonic than polyphonic.
3. Phrases are usually shorter.
4. The rhythm is more measured and less plastic.
5. It is usually accompanied, whereas the motet is usually sung *a cappella*.

The anthem is a notable contribution to church music and not a latter-day degeneration of motet style. Furthermore, since the anthem is created in the English language, it has a unique appropriateness for English-speaking churches, all things else being equal. The anthems of Tye, Tallis, Byrd, Purcell, and Handel are worthy of high places in our practice of music. Unfortunately, the market is flooded with anthems of later periods, when the anthem style had deteriorated.

17

Solo Song

There is a reluctance in liturgical Churches today to admit the propriety of the use of solos in the worship service. This reluctance is expressed in some churches by an outright ban upon solos, and in others by a quiet despair in the presence of a "necessary evil."

It is difficult to find any historical justification for this point of view. The use of soloists in liturgical worship has been a feature of the Church's music since time immemorial. In Jewish and ancient and medieval Christian worship there was the cantor, who sang alone and was responded to (but not accompanied by) the choir. In the fourteenth century there was a large production of solo motets with instrumental accompaniment. One of the distinguishing features of the Baroque motet (1600—1750) was the abandonment of the *a cappella* style of Palestrina and others, and the addition of accompaniment and solo passages. The solo cantatas of Buxtehude and others are another contribution of the Baroque era. The so-called "verse anthems" of England are anthems in which solo stanzas are alternated with choral stanzas.

The most frequently used argument against the use of solos is this: In the worship service the whole body of believers is worshiping. It is an intrusion upon this community of worship for a "star" singer to arise and, by singing a solo, introduce a personal and theatrical element. This argument has merit *if* the solo is used personally and theatrically. The history noted above would indicate, however, that such use is not an inevitable concomitant of solo singing. It is perfectly possible for a solo to be used and presented in such a manner as to aid rather than hinder the worship of all present.

The historical and liturgical objections to the solo are not the real objections. In the opinion and experience of the writer the difficulty lies in three directions:

1. The attitude of singer and people.
2. The material.
3. The manner of presentation.

If the attitude of the singer is a personal one, if his aim is to impress *himself*, rather than *God*, upon the people, then indeed the solo is out of place. If, however, the soloist is made aware of his real function, which is to bring the message of grace to his hearers and to lead them in worship and praise, there can be no more objection to his presence than to the presence of the liturgist and organist, who are also soloists of a sort.

The antipathy toward solos is supported most strongly by the type of song often chosen by soloists. Many "church solos" are really only ballads with religious (and sometimes only semi-religious) texts. The style of the music is so personal, so sensual, so humanly dramatic, that the solo jars the sensitive spirit. Here indeed is a valid objection to the solo — if music of this type is used. To ban solos on this basis, however, is to state that no suitable music exists. This is simply not true. Many of the solo cantatas, motets, and anthems previously alluded to are perfectly suited to the worship service. A simple chorale or hymn with or without a special accompaniment is always very much in place.

The manner of presentation by the soloist is the most difficult of the factors to regulate. The average vocal teacher teaches his pupils to emphasize and project their personalities. He does this because he has the concert stage, radio, and television in mind, and he assumes the same set of standards for the church. The result is that the average "trained singer" is a mugger, a waver of arms, a dramatic dropper of music, a soulful looker at the audiences and the heavens above, a banshee on high notes and a mouse on low. This is, of course, very comic and deplorable. But it is not necessary or inevitable if the church takes the trouble to train the soloist.

Here lies the crux of the situation: Many churches and musicians have assumed that soloists as a class are unanimously intractable and unteachable. Some are, as are some other people. But a pastor and a musician, working together, can work wonders in the minds and attitudes of these singers if the special demands of the worship service are made meaningful for them. They will even find it a special joy to take extra trouble in choosing their music and otherwise preparing themselves to perform this highest act of the soloist. A few instructions regarding their demeanor while singing will usually take care of offensive mannerisms, and a planned program of solos for the year, selected by the musician, will offer an excellent opportunity to discuss the special requirements of the music of the church.

It is obviously not our purpose to suggest that the solo should be the basic special vocal song of the church. The congregation and the choir are still and must remain the principal vocal groups in worship. But it is foolish to restrict the possibilities of worship experiences in *any* direction for light or insufficient cause. The solo, judiciously and reverently prepared and sung, can contribute, as the history and experience of the Church abundantly reveal.

CHAPTER 4

Instrumental Music in Worship

THE history of the use of instruments in worship presents a cloudy and contradictory picture. There has never been any question about the fitness of vocal music for worship; even the most extreme Calvinists permitted and even encouraged the congregation to sing hymns. But instrumental music, unless in accompaniment of singing, is divorced to a greater or lesser degree from the Word and has therefore often been looked upon as having an exclusively sensuous and theatrical appeal. Furthermore, most instruments have been historically more commonly used in secular and popular connotations than in religious, and the Church has been properly jealous of the sanctity of the sanctuary.

We are faced here, therefore, with a twofold problem: (1) Can music which has at best a secondary relation to the Word of God be admitted into the service? and (2) To what extent ought the Church forego the use of instruments on the ground that these instruments have a primarily secular use and connotation?

In the practice of music among the Jews we have ample evidence from the Scriptures that instrumental music was freely used. A number of instruments are referred to, among them trumpets, organs, and cymbals. Some of the instruments were even taken over into the Temple service from Egyptian and no doubt other pagan sources. Among these were a large harp, the lyre, and the oboe. The implication is very strong that it is not the instrument itself or the tone which it produces, but rather its use which sanctifies it for the praise of God.

Medieval Christian practice presents a different picture. The early Church Fathers warned against the use of instruments in public worship because they were used by pagans in orgiastic "religious" rites, by warriors, and in frivolous and sensuous popular music. What apparently had happened is that the predominant use of instruments even in the Christian community had passed from the Christian Church and entered the service of secularism and worse.

At the time of the Reformation, instruments were used freely in church services. The organ was as yet not highly developed or universally used, but strings, lutes, flutes, trumpets, and trombones were. Bach, of course, used the harpsichord and/or organ and a small orchestra in accompaniment of his cantatas.

American practice today has inherited, in addition to the inconclusive picture presented above, the Calvinistic feeling that instrumental music, simply because it is pleasing to the ear, is therefore out of place in worship. This feeling has been moderated to permit at least the organ to enter the church, but it still maintains a rather effective ban upon other instruments among American Protestants generally.

From all of this the following conclusions seem admissable: (1) God has not forbidden the use of instruments in public worship, but rather has in the Psalms and in the inspired pattern of Jewish worship encouraged their use. (2) The experience of the Church indicates, however, that secular, immoral, and even blasphemous practices can invade the Church through instrumental music. For this reason the Church must carefully consider the materials and instruments used, and their probable effect upon worship. An example in present-day terms would be a saxophone rendition of "Home on the Range" or "I Love You Truly" in a service of worship. The instrument in question is used primarily in the dance hall, the tunes mentioned are secular, and the probable effect upon the people would hardly be worshipful.

Beyond this obvious example, however, there are two further and much more subtle dangers in the use of instrumental music. One is the fact that instrumental music can easily become completely divorced from the Word and develop a life of its own extrinsic to the rest of worship. It is not necessary that every piece of instrumental music be based upon a hymn, chorale, or liturgical melody. But it is necessary that every piece of such music be related in mood and be calculated to support and unify rather than interrupt the service.

We can conclude, therefore, with reference to the first problem posed at the beginning of this chapter, that pure instrumental music can be permitted in the worship service on either or both of the following conditions:

1. That it is based upon a tune which is familiar to the congregation and which has the capacity to remind them of the Word of God.

2. That it is related in mood to the mood of the service and does not introduce secular or otherwise foreign elements.

In the chapter on the selection and presentation of instrumental music these points will be further discussed.

The second danger is that instrumental music presents the same

21

kind of temptation as does solo song. The temptation is to entertain and/or to exhibit special technical achievements. We are not here speaking of concerts in the church, in which more difficult and culturally more challenging music may properly be heard. In the worship service, however, the music ought to be simple and relatively unobtrusive. If the people upon leaving the service comment particularly upon the excitement and interest of the music, the musician has *failed*. This is perhaps not a popular opinion among musicians, but it is nevertheless profoundly true. Music is to serve the Gospel; its position is that of a servant. The danger of transgressing this boundary is always imminent, but its imminence is most threatening in the case of instrumental music.

The Organ

The unanimity with which the organ has been accepted as the chief musical instrument in the public worship of Western Christendom makes it surprising to discover that the organ is a latecomer to the sanctuary. As late as the mid-16th century Luther took little note of the organ as a worship instrument, since the service in his day was almost entirely vocal. It is true that the organ is mentioned in the Psalms, but only as one among many instruments, and by no means the chief.

The reason for this low estimate of the organ in earlier times is undoubtedly to be found in part in the fact that the organ as then developed was a clumsy and often raucous-sounding instrument, while other instruments were more highly developed. Another factor which caused churchmen to look with some suspicion upon the organ was the practice of many organists of using music based upon secular and even licentious song in the service. It may be difficult for us to imagine such a practice, but it was carried on not only in organ music, but also, as we have noted, in some medieval motets in which the actual words of love songs and other popular ditties were brought into the church. A third reason was probably the undeveloped state of the science of notation. It was comparatively easy to notate a single line of melody for instruments such as the flute, viol, or trumpet, but it was quite another matter to notate all the parts possible and desirable for organ music in the crude systems of notation then in use.

Whatever the reasons, however, the organ has only in the last three centuries assumed its dominant position in the music of the church.

Today it is considered virtually unthinkable to conduct public worship without the organ.

HISTORY

A brief examination of the history of the organ will help to illuminate some aspects of the relationship between the organ and worship. The construction of the first organ is generally ascribed to the Greek engineer Ktesibios who lived in Alexandria around 250 B. C. (This refers to a record of an actual instrument whose principles are known. The reference to organs in the Bible may or may not denote an instrument whose principles are similar to those of the modern organ.) His instrument was called a hydraulis and was based upon principles which were generally known in his time. It contained the earmarks of an organ, i. e., it had a mechanically produced wind supply which acted upon pipes by means of a key. Because of its loud and raucous tone it became associated in Roman culture with gladiator contests and orgiastic rites. Until the year 1300 the organ changed little in musical character or mechanical adequacy. Obviously it could not well be used by the Church.

Around 1300, however, new organs were developed which were small enough to be used in churches and homes. The tones produced by these organs were also softer, better developed harmonically, and more varied in color. With steadily improving mechanism it also became possible to play more easily and to play many voices simultaneously.

By 1500 the organ had begun to replace the chanting of some parts of the liturgy with preludes based upon the chant. In the Church of the Reformation these preludes and voluntaries gradually came to be based upon the chorale rather than upon plainchant tunes, and thus there arose the glorious literature of chorale preludes which still forms the core of all organ music.

The organs which were produced in the 17th and 18th centuries are considered to be tonally the finest organs ever built. They were built to play effectively the polyphonic music of Pachelbel, Buxtehude, Bach, and the many others of this school, and hence had a bright, clear, easily differentiated tone.

In the 19th and early 20th centuries organ-building suffered a serious decline into romanticism which paralleled the romantic movement in composition and did great harm to the organ as an instrument. The difficulty arose primarily from a romantic and sentimental approach to music generally, and from a misconception of the organ. The romantic movement in art emphasized expression of self and heightening of personalized emotions. This led organ builders to create stops such as the celestes, vox humana, and devices such as the tremulant and swell shade which were calculated to give the organ greater personal "expressiveness." The emphasis in organ playing came to be placed not so much upon the music and its spiritual origin and content as upon the manner in which the individual organist expressed his feelings about the music. In church art, whether musical or otherwise, rampant individualism leads to confusion and decay. While the devices and stops named above have their legitimate (but limited) uses, it can fairly be said that their emphasis is unfair both to worship and to the organ itself.

The misconception regarding the organ which arose during the romantic period was that the organ was an orchestra. It isn't, of course; it is different in so many musical and technical ways that the difference is obvious. Nevertheless, from this basic misconception came the attempt to imitate orchestral sounds in the individual voices of the organ. Trumpets, flutes, strings, and reeds were voiced in imitation of their orchestral counterparts. The result was a sentimental, heavy, clumsy instrument which did not lend itself at all to the playing of characteristic polyphonic organ music. The organ was often superficially pleasing in some of its individual voices, but the ensemble effect was muddy and indecisive. The tone soon palled upon the ear, and musical people in droves fled the excruciating tonal experience.

In the past 25 years a reaction against the romantic organ has set in. Leading organ builders are taking voluntary instruction from the great organs of Bach's time. As is usually the case with revivals, it is virtually impossible to transfer from one era to another all the variable factors which determine the result. Some of the so-called "Baroque" organs being produced by contemporary builders are shrill and hard in the extreme. To counteract the romantic conception of "pretty" tone, some have built organs in which the individual tones are aggressively unpleasant. Some others have been indifferent to the technical advances of the period of the romantic organ, an attitude which seems violently foolish. Nevertheless, the best of what might be termed American classic organs are indeed a notable achievement in returning to the organ its past glory and even improving it, if that is possible, as a great instrument of religious expression. The new instruments have a clear, bright, easily produced tone and at the same time a full-throated ensemble of authentic organ grandeur. These organs promise a new day in the world of organ music, playing, and construction, and in particular a new and corrected emphasis upon the place of the organ in worship.

24

Here we must also briefly mention the very recent development of electronic "organs." If by the term "organ" we mean an instrument which produces its tone by means of a controlled wind pressure acting upon a pipe by means of a key, then these electronic instruments are not organs. It is also true that even untrained ears can tell the tonal difference between an electronic and a real organ, particularly in support of congregational singing, where the organ should be at its best, and the electronic is at its worst. Many small churches have resorted to the use of electronic instruments because they are cheaper than organs. We would almost always suggest the temporary use of a piano until a small organ can be bought. Whatever may be the uses of electronic instruments, their synthetic-sounding tone and lack of a full-bodied ensemble make them inappropriate for really vigorous and satisfying worship.

FUNCTION IN WORSHIP

What has been said in general of the function of instruments in worship necessarily applies here also. There are, however, a few other considerations which apply particularly to the organ, since it is overwhelmingly the chief instrument of the worship service.

The primary function of the organ in worship is the support of congregational singing both in liturgy and hymnody. This is the most important consideration both for the builder and the player. The organ may, by its tonal design, be rendered capable of doing many things, but unless it can lead the congregation surely, clearly, and with life and spirit, it will be a failure. The player must also keep in mind that the chief excellence demanded of him is the ability to lead the congregation in its part of the service.

Secondly, the organ is used to unify the various parts of the service. More will be said on this point in a later and more detailed chapter, but we here briefly note that the organ may properly be expected to keep the service flowing evenly without halts, hitches, and dead spots. It can serve to blend together the various religious attitudes of prayer, praise, entreaty, and gratitude.

In the third place, the organ through the usual "solo" opportunities in the service — the prelude, voluntary, and postlude — serves to emphasize the message of the service at the beginning, in the middle immediately after the sermon, and at the very end. We might also include here other features which have a more technical than functional aspect, such as modulation and accompaniment. All of these matters are deferred to later chapters.

CHAPTER 5

Playing the Music of the Liturgy

WITH this chapter we enter that portion of our discussion which deals with the practical problems of the church musician as he sits at his console and faces his choir in the service. It will be our purpose to translate into practice, in so far as this is possible on paper, the general principles laid down in preceding chapters.

By the word liturgy we here mean those parts of the service other than set organ pieces, hymns, choral or solo songs, and sermon, in other words, that part of the worship which is often called the "order of service." Our discussion will treat primarily of the "Order of the Holy Communion" found in *The Lutheran Hymnal* of the Synodical Conference, copyright 1941, on pages 15 to 31.

The Lutheran Church is a "liturgical" church; that is, it maintains in its services the order of worship which was developed in the Middle Ages. Many Protestant church bodies in our country and elsewhere have dispensed in part or altogether with the traditional parts of the ancient Mass, or Holy Communion service, and one finds merely a call to worship, Scripture readings, hymns, solos and anthems, a sermon, and distribution of Holy Communion. Luther, however, and the Lutheran Church after him, saw good reason to retain all that was good both in doctrine and practice in the Catholic faith, and so the Lutheran liturgy follows very closely upon the Catholic Mass.[9]

In brief, the service outline is as follows:

The Preparation (from the Prelude until the Introit).

The Office of the Word (from the Introit through the Sermon).

The Offerings (the Offertory, Offerings, and Prayers).

The Preface and Sanctus (an intermediate part connecting the Offerings and the Communion).

[9] For a fuller discussion of the Lutheran service and its antecedents, see F. R. Webber, *Studies in the Liturgy* (Erie, Pa.: Ashby Printing Co., 1938), and Luther D. Reed, *The Lutheran Liturgy*, rev. ed. (Philadelphia: Muhlenberg Press, 1960).

The Communion.

The Post-Communion (from the celebration of Communion through the Postlude).

The various items included within this general framework are calculated to make the worshiper aware of his natural sinful condition, to bring him the good news of God's free grace in Christ, and to apply this grace to the individual worshiper in the most personal way possible by means of Holy Communion. The two books mentioned in the footnote offer excellent and complete discussions of the meaning of the various liturgical items in the service, which we shall not repeat here. Our aim is rather to offer suggestions as to how the service may be well led by the organist.

The most obvious thing which will impress anyone who takes the time to look closely at the liturgy is that there is a progression and flow of thought towards the Word and the Sacrament. In the Preparation there is a confession of the need for the Word and Sacrament; in the Office of the Word there is a humble and yet happy anticipation of the Word and also its presentation in readings and sermon; in the Offerings there is joyful and prayerful response to the announcement of God's grace; in the Preface and Sanctus there is a note of jubilant anticipation of the Sacrament; in the Communion all the benefits of God's grace are once more offered and sealed unto us, this time individually; and finally the service ends in the jubilant songs and responses of the Nunc Dimittis and Thanksgiving. There is here a very apparent completeness and unity.

Simply stated, the organist's function is to preserve and support this unity and progression. He should strive for an even flow from part to part; there should be no awkward and unwarranted pauses; there should be a vigorous and steady progression in the music as well as in the thought of the liturgy.

Just how this can be achieved in each individual situation is of course a question so dependent upon the variable factors in the situation that only a few very general directions can possibly be attempted.

1. Pace or tempo:

    a. The liturgy is essentially a reflective conversation between God and congregation. The tempo of the individual parts is the tempo of speech. The pace should be unhurried and thoughtful. Too fast a movement gives the impression of carelessness; too slow a movement robs the liturgy of its joyous character.

27

b. The organ must establish and maintain the tempo. If the organ is exactly with the singing in time, or slightly behind, the singing will drag. The organ must be imperceptibly ahead of the singing.

2. Volume of organ tone:

   a. It will be obvious that the organist should not use the same volume of organ tone throughout the liturgy. The volume should at all times, however, be forceful enough to lead. Never require the people to guess whether or when they are to sing. The full volume of tone used must be present on the first chord of any one section.

   b. The shorter responses are usually played with a more subdued registration, while longer sections are generally more brilliant. Save full organ for the Glorias, Sanctus, and Nunc Dimittis. Do not play too softly for the Agnus Dei and the Offertory.

   c. The range from soft to loud should not be great; it should imply rather than state the difference in thought and purpose between the various sections.

   d. The practice of varying the volume within a longer liturgical song is not a good one, i. e., in the Gloria in Excelsis and Sanctus. These are units in themselves.

3. Character of organ tone:

   The registration used for the liturgy is necessarily dependent upon the organ, the acoustical properties of the church, and the number of people present. The character of the liturgy is an essentially joyful one, and for this reason a gloomy collection of dull 8′ stops is the worst possible registration. In general the tone quality should be bright and firm. Remember that the congregation supplies the 8′ tone — the normal pitch. You cannot lead a congregation's singing well by building up a powerful concentration of 8′ stops, because the organ then plays at the same level as that at which the congregation sings. Adding power will depress the singing. Rather, use clear diapasons at 8′ and 4′ pitches, and add such other tones as are clear and steady. Occasionally vary the tone color by the addition and the subtraction of particularly the higher-pitched stops, such as 4′, 2⅔′, 2′, and mixtures.

4. Much of the liturgy is syllabic. Sometimes, however, reciting tones are used, in which case there are two or more words to one note, as in the Gloria in Excelsis. Do not beat the reciting note by repeating it for each word of the text. Repetition of the note slows the chanting and interrupts its flow.

Frequently organists, as well as others interested in the musical practices of the Church, become impatient or disappointed that there is a lack of uniformity within the Church as to liturgy. Some congregations use the entire liturgy as it appears in the hymnbook; some alter or reduce it to fit local circumstances. There are probably few congregations which do not at some place or other consistently sing a wrong note or sing it out of its proper rhythm. So long as these variants do not rob the people of worship experiences meaningful to them, they are inconsequential and indeed serve to emphasize something quite important. Uniformity in liturgical practice has never been an aim of the Lutheran Church. Luther himself fashioned several orders of service and permitted variations within these. Liturgical practice is a part of church life within the province of the individual congregation to decide.

This is not to say, however, that the church musician should do nothing in the face of liturgical incompleteness and crudity. It is his responsibility, together with the pastor, to suggest and provide ever greater and more significant worship experiences to the people, so that here, too, they may grow in grace. To this end we should use the church's educational agencies, the various organizations within the congregation, and occasionally also a few minutes before or after the service, to explain and practice parts of the liturgy which are new to the people or which they sing poorly.

CHAPTER 6

The Playing of Hymns

CHORALES and hymns occupy a position of centrality in Lutheran worship and Protestant worship generally which is difficult to over-emphasize. As previously noted, Luther gave chorales an integral place in worship when he used them to replace various parts of the liturgy. Chorales and hymns serve also to teach the truths of God in an easily remembered form, and they offer an opportunity for the congregation to reflect and ponder. Added to these values is the historical fact that the chorale has been the basic material of the great mass of great instrumental and vocal music produced from Luther's time to Bach's. It is clear that the importance of the chorale (and the hymn second-arily) both as a liturgical unit and as an art form must be appraised in the highest terms.

Since it is in the chorales and hymns that the music of the Church comes closest to the average worshiper, it is of the utmost importance that the organist be able to accompany hymns supremely well. Hymn playing is not the easiest thing the organist does. It re-quires a certain degree of technical competence and facility and a large measure of discrimination and taste.

Technique

Technically, the organist must strive to play *with* rather than *for* the congregation. The ideal accompaniment results when organ and congregation are welded into one unit. The tempo must be vigorous, steady, and sharply rhythmical. The volume of organ tone should be great enough to support and inspire, but not so loud as to overpower.

The average worshiper wants two things from the organist in hymn playing: a clear indication as to how and when he is to proceed, and a constant flow of organ tone to support his singing, which he is rather afraid is none too good. To supply these needs, the following technical rule should be observed in playing hymns: *All notes are to be played legato or tied, except repeated melody notes.* Examples 1A and 1B on page 32 will serve to illustrate the rule.

There are two principal exceptions to this rule:

1. If more than two beats of a measure in 4/4 rhythm have the same bass note, strike the bass note on counts one and three. See Example 2 on pages 32 and 33.

2. At the beginning of some hymns where the entire chord is repeated, it is well to restrike the entire chord so that a strong rhythm is immediately established. See Example 3 on page 33.

Phrasing is a technical problem which does not lend itself to hard and fast definition. Phrases are variously indicated in hymnals, some using the fermata, and others, heavy perpendicular lines of varying lengths, as does the *Lutheran Hymnal.* In general, the longer perpendicular lines in the *Lutheran Hymnal* indicate the end of a complete phrase, and the shorter lines indicate a "lift" in the melody at the end of a half-phrase or motive. Neither the fermata nor the black lines are intended to mean a "hold" or interruption in the rhythm. The organist must keep the tempo going. To make a complete stop at each fermata or line is to break the melody and text into little bits which do not hang together. It makes for slow, uninspiring singing. We cannot here go into the many instances where the above general rule must be somewhat modified. The only way to learn to play hymns successfully is to listen critically when they are played and sung by others, and then to sing them to oneself in preparation for playing. If the organist will remember to keep the tempo moving ahead and to think of the long phrase rather than the half-phrase or motive, he will not go far wrong.

Example 1a

Hymn 287, *The Lutheran Hymnal*

Written:

Example 1b

Played:

Example 2

Hymn 647, *The Lutheran Hymnal*

Written:

Played:

Example 3

Hymn 36, *The Lutheran Hymnal*

Written:

Played:

Artistic Considerations

It is in the area of taste and emotion, however, that the organist makes his chief contribution to hymn singing. He can by means of registration and tempo so clarify the meaning of the hymn and uncover its emotional drive that the congregation is, as it were, lifted beyond itself. This is an art which defies description and which cannot be achieved simply by following a set of directions, but it is an authentic and necessary part of service playing and one of the great values of hymnody.

INTRODUCING THE HYMN

The first step in securing effective participation in hymn singing is the introduction to the hymn.

Historically and practically the best method of introducing any chorale or hymn is to play or improvise a short prelude on its theme, which serves to lead the congregation's thoughts into the thoughts of the hymn. This practice has largely fallen into disuse because it tends to lengthen the service beyond a point acceptable to a contemporary

33

American congregation and because, except for preludes on the chorales, few preludes of real value or suitability exist for the ordinary hymns. Then, too, the art of improvisation is largely a lost one today, and organists are fearful of disturbing the service with ill-planned fantasies. A revival of the practice of preludizing is very much in order, however, since by this method the organist can most fully prepare the congregation for its important function. A revival of the art of simple improvisation and the writing of short, simple preludes on hymns and chorales are two much-needed developments.

The simplest method of introducing the hymn is to play it on the Swell organ with or without pedal. It should be played in exactly the same tempo at which it is to be sung, and even the pause between introduction and singing should be counted out exactly, so that there is a strong rhythm created which will serve to unify the singing and give it life. At the end of the introduction, during a slight pause, the player merely adds a stop or a coupler to the pedal and plays for the congregation on the Great manual, which is registered stronger than the Swell.

Another method, to be used for variety and usually only for hymns other than chorales, is to play the melody on a solo combination, the alto and tenor in the left hand on an accompanying soft combination, and the bass in the pedal. This method requires a bit of practice in reading and also considerable dexterity in changing the organ rapidly during the pause between introduction and singing. The latter problem is solved easily if the organ is equipped with pistons. If not, the player must play a close on the Swell at the end of the introduction (an elongated "Amen" will do) during which time he can arrange the stops on the Great manual. This method should be used sparingly so that its variety value is retained.

REGISTRATION

Registration is an art analogous to the choice and use of color by a painter. The organist usually has a reasonably complete set of tone colors available. The vitality and effectiveness of his congregation's hymn singing will depend to a great extent upon his artistic manipulation of these colors. Here again we must warn that great art is simple, but subtle; the degree of variation in loudness and color should be fairly narrow. Obviously sensational changes from fortissimo to pianissimo are ludicrous and totally out of keeping with the reverence necessary for worship. Nevertheless it will immediately be felt that one cannot

34

use the same registration for both "A Mighty Fortress" and "O Sacred Head, Now Wounded."

Specific instruction in the choice of stops is as impossible to give here as it was in the case of the liturgy, and for the same reasons. The general rules there noted apply also here. There is, however, one additional point to be mentioned which arises out of the fact that hymnody, unlike liturgy, is strophic. Since the same music is repeated several times, and since also the thought of each stanza is usually somewhat different from the others, it sometimes becomes artistically desirable to vary the registration slightly in one or several stanzas. Again it must be warned that this technique should be used sparingly and subtly. Too great or frequent changes will disturb the essential unity of the hymn. A case in point is Hymn 38, "The Lord, My God, Be Praised." Note that the first three stanzas enumerate the works of the three Persons of the Trinity; the fourth is a summary and also points to the praises sung by the heavenly host. These four stanzas are really reflective in essence. Only in the fifth does the congregation itself fully join all creation in a full-bodied song of praise. Rather than to play this entire hymn on full organ, it would be artistically and emotionally much more fitting to hold the last several ounces of power in reserve until the last stanza, and only then to add the final crowning tones.

OTHER DEVICES

Among other devices which can be used (sparingly, please) are the following:

1.   Play an occasional stanza on the manuals only. This practice affords a welcome relief from the constant droning 16′ pedal sound.

2.   Have the congregation sing an occasional stanza without organ accompaniment. It is advisable to use this device only if the congregation has been warned that it is about to happen, and the choir has been alerted to lead.

3.   An ancient Lutheran practice is that of alternation. The congregation sings a stanza; then the choir sings one a cappella, perhaps in parts; the organ may take another stanza later without any singing. Here, too, one must in some way announce the order to be followed.

4.   Organ and choir descants may be used at times for the purpose of securing variety and in order to heighten musical effectiveness. They are of doubtful value since the result, in the writer's expe-

35

rience at least, is that the congregation usually sings more softly in order to listen. Thus the purpose of the descant — to increase the singing effort — is nullified. If, on the other hand, the descant has become well known or is expected, the singing is usually somewhat aided.

All these devices, and any others that might be thought of, are only that — devices. They are not the substance of hymn playing. They are spices, not food. They must be used as a great cook might delicately use the most exotic condiments, but they must not be offered as the meal. The danger in them is the old and ever-present one that the music can so easily replace God in the service. We remember a conversation with a musically sensitive person who had attended a service in a certain church. The organ, he reported, was forever *doing* something. No hymn was played straight through without variation; registration throughout the service was extreme and dramatic; the choir jumped in at all sorts of unlikely places. Our friend left the service extremely conscious of the musician, but spiritually and emotionally upset. That musician failed in that service, because he showed the people himself, when they had come to see God.

Ultimately, the effective playing of hymns will not be determined by a technical grasp of all the devices possible, but by an understanding and believing heart. If the organist will seek to be in sympathy with God, with the occasion, with the hymn, and with his people, he will over a period of time develop the necessary artistic discrimination to do also this service supremely well.

RELATED PROBLEMS

The "Amen" is to be sung by the congregation at the close of hymns which contain prayer or praise. If the hymn is primarily reflective or didactic, omit the "Amen."

"Enriching" the harmony of the hymn by the addition of frequent passing-tones and dominant seventh chords is to be discouraged. Unless the organist is exceedingly well trained in harmony, he is best advised to stick to the printed page. The gifted and well-trained organist will not have to be told how he can artistically vary the harmony.

Complete instructions for the use of the Swell shades in hymn playing: Don't!

Complete instructions for the use of the tremolo in hymn playing: Especially don't!

36

CHAPTER 7

The Choice and Presentation of Vocal Music

Choice

IN this chapter we shall treat of the vocal music of the service other than hymns and liturgy; in other words, the music sung by the choir or a soloist. The choice of this music is determined first of all by a consideration of its value for the praise of God. It cannot be said too often or too emphatically that a true service of worship is God-centered, not man-centered. The musician must forever ask himself this question: "Are we offering God the very best of which the choir and I are capable?" Secondly, the choice of music is determined by a consideration of its suitability for the particular service in which it is to be used. This is true of all the music heard in a service, including the hymns. Ordinarily the hymns are chosen by the pastor to fit the message of the service and particularly also of the sermon. The musician usually begins his task of filling out the musical portions of the service after the hymns have been chosen. In the third place the music must be chosen for its ability to communicate to the hearers. This is a problem not of quality, but of language. Not every group of people will be able at once to understand every worthwhile musical language. It is the duty of the musician patiently and lovingly to develop the needed understandings by the use of the best examples of whatever musical language is employed.

LITURGICAL MATERIALS

In recent years the chanting of the Introit and the Gradual by the choir has been revived by many of our churches. This is a movement to be encouraged because it has, in many cases, returned these two parts of the liturgy to services which had altogether dropped them. Their choice presents no problem to the musician, since they are definitely prescribed and appointed for all services of the church year.

The texts of these and other liturgical parts are to be found in the *Lutheran Hymnal* on pages 54 to 101. Concordia Publishing House has also published Gregorian settings of the Introits and Anglican and Gregorian settings of the Graduals in two excellent books: *The Introits for the Church Year* and *The Graduals for the Church Year*. Several variants are possible for the Gradual. One may have the choir sing a seasonal sentence, sequence hymn, or motet or anthem, or the congregation may sing an appropriate hymn.

THE MOTET AND ANTHEM

The singing of a special musical selection by the choir or soloist is a practice which has ample justification in both the history of the Church and in proper liturgical practice. We have noted in Chapter 3 that the Church has always intended that its musical life be not bound by the limitations of simple congregational song. The anthem or motet has a legitimate and important function in the service.

Its function is, however, one of liturgical character, not of entertainment. When the anthem is chosen simply to entertain or to fill in time, it disrupts the unity which has been so carefully built up by the liturgy and the hymns. The first criterion in the choice of anthems therefore is fitness for the praise of God in the particular service in question. To determine this, the choirmaster must consult the Introit and the Gradual of the day, the hymns chosen by the pastor, the Gospel and Epistle lessons, and the text, and if possible, the main emphasis of the sermon. This can obviously be fully done only if the pastor plans his program at least a month ahead and informs the musician promptly.

The place of the special musical number should be carefully chosen to emphasize and utilize its liturgical nature. The two best places are usually between the Gospel and the Epistle (in place of the Gradual), and immediately after the Creed before the office hymn.

Purely musical considerations should never be the primary or determining factors in the choice of music for the service, but they nevertheless play an important role in any carefully planned program. We have discussed in Chapter 3 the main fields from which spiritually and musically significant materials can be drawn. The Lutheran Church is the fortunate inheritor of a distinctive musical legacy which it is difficult to overvalue. In the chorale and the music built on the chorale we have a literature of great significance spiritually and of tremendous power and meaning musically. The Lutheran musician will strongly emphasize this heritage in his selection, and not merely because it is

Lutheran, but primarily because it is vital and appropriate for liturgical Lutheran worship.

A sectarian approach, however, would be disastrous. If we are, as we believe and say, not a splinter sect theologically, but rather an integral part of the entire Church of Christ on earth, then we have little justification for using nothing but the chorale and its surrounding material. The Lutheran Church has a tradition which predates Luther — a musical tradition which Luther himself pointedly emphasized when he advocated the use of Gregorian chant and praised highly such Roman Catholic composers as Josquin and Senfl.

Unfortunately, from the musical standpoint, materials produced in the 19th and early 20th centuries cannot stand muster with the products mentioned above. The music even of such great composers as Brahms and Mendelssohn is too personal and romantically over-stuffed and pretty for much use in the service. The lesser lights, such as Sullivan and Stainer, are merely vapid. In recent years, however, there has been a return to fine contrapuntal writing for the Church, a return which it can be hoped may lead to a vigorous new school of church composition.

It is from these three fields, then: Gregorian chant and motet, Lutheran chorale and motet, and very recent works, that the church musician will be best advised to draw his materials.

One of the most difficult aspects of choosing vocal music for the service is the problem of congregational response. Music is chosen primarily for the worship and praise of God, but it is an inescapable corollary that if the music is foreign to the experiences of the worshipers, they cannot worship through it. Here the art of the musician is taxed to the greatest degree. How shall he give to his people the great treasures of the music of the Church in the face of their inability to understand the message in the particular language used?

The answer lies in the area of teaching. It must be remembered that the ability to understand and appreciate anything beyond the most superficial aspect of things requires effort. The musician must keep in mind that his congregation has not shared his opportunity to find the beauties lying within the music of the Church. It is also a fact, however, and a most comforting one, that most choir members and lay people are open-minded, willing, and even eager to improve and deepen their understanding. If the musician will take the trouble to explain, to show, to reveal the beauties of his materials, all but a few die-hards will eventually participate gladly in the finest music the Church has produced. The level of appreciation can be raised, given time, patience, and an unwavering dedication.

THE SOLO

What has been said in Chapter 3 regarding the solo, and what has been said above regarding the anthem or motet, applies here also. The difficulties are somewhat magnified because of the origin of the music which most soloists have in their repertoire. Most soloists use materials which are really operatic arias or love songs set to religious words. To introduce to them liturgically and musically more fitting materials is not an easy task. In recent years, however, much fine solo material has been reissued. Offer this to the soloists. In addition, do not overlook the possibilities of the solo anthem and the ordinary hymn or chorale, whether or not in a special setting.

The catalog, bulletins, and examination packages of Concordia Publishing House comprise the finest and most complete service to the choirmaster in the task of finding suitable choral and solo materials. The music presented is of a high quality and is so chosen as to fit the needs of soloists and all types of choral organizations. The writer recommends that these services and the services of other publishers be used for the purpose of securing specific materials suitable in each particular case.

Presentation

We are living in an age which is artistically style-conscious. We speak of "period" furniture and distinguish it sharply from "modern." Some of our greatest contemporary artists are notable chiefly for their style, not for their meaning. Hence abstractionist art, which eschews all meaning. What is left is only a sensory experience in the use of color, line, and mass. The music of the Church has not escaped this unbalanced pre-occupation with style. The average *a cappella* concert of religious music is careful to present many styles of music, but frequently overlooks, both in selection and presentation, the message without which no artistic experience is complete or satisfying. Hence also the overcultured tone quality in many choirs, the attempted imitation of orchestral color, the exaggerated "effects" which the suffering music is asked to bear.

And yet "style," correctly appraised, is an important means of securing communication between musicians and congregation. We shall consider it briefly in relation to the types of music mentioned above as being the chief materials for Christian worship in our day.

Liturgical chant and liturgical motet, by their inherent avoidance of extremes in pitch and dynamics, do not lend themselves to exuberant, dramatic presentation. In fact, most performances of this material do not err on this side, but on the opposite: on the side of indefiniteness and vagueness. Performances of this material often give only a filmy and mystic effect, which in connection with votive candles and a darkened sanctuary passes for religion in some circles. It must be remembered that also this material is intended to nourish the hearers spiritually, not to anaesthetize them into a dream state.

The term "chanting" is used to denote the presentation of unison liturgical music in the Psalms, Introit, and, in part, the Gradual. Probably the most difficult feature in chanting is rhythm, because it is the rhythm of speech, not the mechanical beat to which we are most accustomed. An untrained choir will tend to sing all syllables on notes of equal time value, which, of course, would not give the tempo of speech. In order to overcome this tendency, it is a good practice to have choirs read the words in chorus first, so that they can hear the verbal stresses. When the chanting is done, these stresses can be referred to. The graduals as presented in the Concordia book of Graduals are set chiefly in Anglican Chant, which is a hybrid between Gregorian and harmonic music. Because of its hybrid character it is not entirely in speech rhythm nor entirely in measured rhythm. Also because of its hybrid character it is sung in four parts rather than in unison.

Motets based upon liturgical chant are not chanted, but sung. It is still true, however, that the rhythm of the singing is not the barred, mechanical rhythm of an anthem. Each phrase in each voice has a rhythm of its own based upon the text in conjunction with its own music. To make this clear, it is necessary to sing each part separately at first so that the climaxes and subordinate parts may be identified and felt. Since the climaxes in all four parts rarely coincide, the musical effect of the whole is a wonderfully subtle flow of music which is constantly changing in color and intensity. Here it is that "style" is important. A heavy-footed approach to the motet utterly destroys its character and beauty and obscures its meaning.

CHORALE AND CHORALE MOTET

The chorale and chorale motet have a radically different sort of meaning and origin and therefore require a radically different type of presentation. It must be remembered that this music is essentially

41

a "people's song," one which by its very purpose cannot make use of the subtleties of chant. The rhythm is much more regular and strong, although still not completely mechanical, the music is syllabic, and there are clearly defined phrases. It is much more forthright, direct, and simple.

For these reasons it is artistically most indefensible to "interpret" the chorale, except in the broadest terms. The practice of running phrases together, or of stopping in the middle of a phrase because a comma happens to pop up, results from a total misunderstanding of the chorale and produces a confusion of style which is painful to one who understands the folk character of this music. It makes no difference that the singing may be done by a highly trained choir. Don't gild the lily! The simple folk character must be maintained, or the chorale is utterly destroyed, and it becomes a pretty plaything.

The chorale motet is distinguished in performance from its liturgical counterpart by the same considerations. Its rhythm is much more vigorous and regular, and its kinship with the people's song is its determining feature. Our purpose is not to argue the superiority of one style over another, but rather to state that the inherent differences dictate a different manner of performance for each. In the singing of chorales and chorale motets, delicacy of nuance in dynamics and tempo is much less evident than in Gregorian music. The emphasis is rather upon clarity and forthrightness.

ANTHEMS AND CONTEMPORARY WORKS

Probably the majority of choral songs heard in the Protestant churches of today would be classified as anthems. As regards performance, the general rules laid down for the chorale motet apply also here. The additional problem created by the fact that most anthems are accompanied we shall discuss in the chapter devoted to accompaniment.

Many contemporary works are in conventional anthem style, but there is today also a welter of other styles and forms being experimented with. The most progressive idioms (such as atonality) are presently still confined to concert music, but both the rhythmic and tonal resources also of service music have recently been somewhat extended. It remains true, however, that the newer compositions for the church service are still quite derivative; i. e., they depend for their success upon a reinterpretation and freshened use of traditional idioms and forms.

Their effective presentation therefore depends upon an analysis of their basic form and style. If there is a rhythmic and tonal flow which suggests Gregorian music, then the manner of chanting or singing such music should be employed. If, on the other hand, the music bears a hymn- or chorale-like quality, that manner should be adopted. What really is needed is the ability to understand the language of the composition, and then the ability to speak it clearly. The musician, to that end, must study his materials carefully and share his understanding with his singers.

Decorum

It should go without saying that the organist, the soloists, and the choristers ought to be models of devotion and propriety in connection with their functions. Engaged as they are upon a sacred task, they must avoid all appearances which might give the lie to their inner dedication. It is for this reason that they properly wear robes in the service. The purpose of robes is to eliminate as much as possible all personally distinguishing features, so that the musicians are represented not as individuals, but rather as a group of people specially dedicated to lead in the worship of God. In fact, even if the choir is located in the west gallery (rear balcony) and is therefore not seen by the congregation, it is a good policy to use robes. The organist and the singers are reminded before every service that their services are directed toward God and that this singing and playing is set apart from all other singing and playing which they do.

The location of the choir and the organ is an important element in decorum. Historically, liturgically, musically, and psychologically the only proper place for the music of the church is in the west gallery. Historically, this was the location of choir and organ in all but the cathedrals and the largest churches. Here the chancel location of the choir resulted from the addition of extra clergy seats, the extra clergymen forming in time a liturgical choir. In all other churches, however, the choir was located in the rear.

Liturgically, the proper position of congregation as well as choir is to face the altar as an expression of the basic fact in worship that all that is done is directed toward God. The necessity which many choirs experience of facing the congregation when they sing has the effect of indicating that their singing is a performance for the congregation and only incidentally for God.

Also musically the west-gallery location gives the best results. When the choir is seated in a side balcony, the voices of many of the

43

singers are not heard directly by many in the congregation. Shoved into a corner, the choral tone does not get a full chance to reverberate in the entire structure and comes out incomplete and lacking resonance. When heard from the rear balcony, however, the tone of the choir has an opportunity to make use of the acoustical properties of the building. It speaks directly into the main body of the church and can, therefore, be most clearly and fully heard by the congregation.

The final advantage of a west-gallery location is psychological. If the organist and the singers are constantly reminded by their position that theirs is an art dedicated to God and not to men, it then becomes much easier to participate with a right spirit within them. To put the choir and the organist on display before the congregation teaches both musicians and congregation that the situation is at least somewhat like that of a concert hall and that the most important thing is to "please" the "audience." This is a far cry indeed from the real situation, which calls for an offering of song to God.

CHAPTER 8

The Choice and Presentation of Organ Music

Choice

ORGANISTS are among the most fortunate of musicians in that there exists for their instrument a literature second to none. From Paumann in the 15th century to Brahms and Franck in the 19th there has been a production of great music in the idiom of the organ. The Lutheran organist is particularly blessed because by general agreement it is recognized that the greatest of this music is that which was produced in the two centuries between Luther and Bach. Furthermore, this music, based primarily upon the Lutheran chorale, was written specifically for the Lutheran service and breathes through its dependence upon the chorale the spirit of Lutheran worship. In fact, the Lutheran organist is almost embarrassed by the amount and value of the material which is available to him, and his problem becomes not one of finding suitable materials, but rather of fitting and adapting them to his needs.

Before the organist can proceed to the task of choosing his organ selections, he must know how they are intended to function and what they are expected to accomplish. In general, the functions of organ pieces in the service are the following:

1. To set or reflect the spirit of the service.
2. To introduce, or reflect upon, a hymn or chorale.
3. To provide a framework for, or to reflect the message of, the Word and sermon.

These three points are really only one, the one point being that organ music never exists for itself in the service, but functions as one of the chief unifying elements. It depends for its validity upon the message and spirit of the service as a whole, the Word, the sermon, and the hymns. Organ music in the service is analogous to the frame of a picture: it is a good and necessary thing, but unimportant except as it serves to point to the picture within.

A thorough understanding of this premise will eliminate much of the music heard in Protestant churches today. On the one hand, it will make apparent the unsuitability of secular songs and sentimentally pretty music. On the other hand, it will restrain the technically proficient organist from using the service as a stage from which to dazzle an audience with his skill. Both extremes are equally wrong; there is no more merit in playing a long and intricate Bach fugue out of its proper setting than there is in playing "Jingle Bells" on Christmas Eve or "Beautiful Isle of Somewhere" to fit a sermon on Heaven.

In our list of functions there is another implication which is frequently debated: Does a piece of organ music have the power to direct the thought and feeling of people to specific verbal concepts? The question is sometimes phrased thus: Can you preach a sermon from the organ? If we take these questions literally, the answer is clearly no. But in a broader sense, it is certainly possible to transmit to a congregation an attitude and spirit which will help to make them receptive to specific ideas. Imagine for a moment the prelude which would be played on Christmas morning, and contrast it in your mind with the prelude you would hear on Good Friday night. On Christmas Day the organist, himself filled with the spirit of joy associated with that day, would play a jubilant prelude based upon a Christmas hymn which would clearly capture and reinforce the joy of the congregation and prepare them for the hearing of the good news. On Good Friday night the prelude would reflect sorrow over the sins which made Good Friday necessary. It would prepare the people to receive the words which tell of the price God paid.

The glory which attaches to the organ in the service is a reflected glory. But there is glory there. It is the glory of being placed into a service higher than itself.

The Choice and Presentation of the Prelude

The function of the prelude in the service is usually twofold: it serves to set the tone of the entire service, and, since the opening hymn usually follows immediately upon it, it serves to introduce the opening hymn. This situation creates somewhat of a problem because the first hymn is often a general morning hymn or hymn of praise which does not specifically point to the message of the day. Nevertheless, because of the close juxtaposition of prelude and first hymn, it is artistically most satisfying if the prelude is chosen to fit the opening hymn as closely as possible. In choosing the prelude the organist must remember that the closest tie between congregation and organist is the hymn, and therefore he should choose the prelude according to the following plan:

1. If possible, play a prelude or improvisation upon the tune and text of the first hymn.

2. If this is not possible, then a prelude or improvisation upon the tune of another hymn in the service, or upon a hymn which is related in sentiment and character to the first hymn.

3. If No. 1 and No. 2 are impossible, then a "non-thematic" prelude, i. e., one which is not based on a hymn tune, but which is related in spirit to the first hymn or to the service as a whole.

The above steps are not intended as a hard and fast rule which must always be mechanically followed. For instance, some preludes on the first hymn of the service may be totally out of keeping with the general spirit of the service, as it is expressed in the various other parts. Then, too, certain practical matters must be taken into consideration. Sometimes the only prelude available is too long, or too short, or the instrument used is inadequate for the piece. Nevertheless the method indicated above is a good general rule to follow, since it asks the musician to consider first of all music which by its theme and character will serve to turn the thoughts of the congregation to the ideas of a hymn to be used in the service.

The following are certain other considerations which enter into the choice and presentation of the prelude:

Length: This will vary according to local practice and specific occasion. In general, a five-minute prelude is long, and, if the organist is not skillful, or too skillful, it is much too long. A one-minute prelude is short for the usual morning service. Length is less important, however, than quality and suitability.

Key: If the prelude is in the same key as the first hymn, you have avoided the necessity of modulating to the key of the first hymn. There is also some artistic value in having the prelude in the same key as the first hymn. No fine and suitable prelude, however, should ever be discarded just because it does not happen to be in the same key as the first hymn. One can sometimes transpose the hymn to suit or use a simple modulation.

Registration: Registration will vary according to the nature of the music and the resources of the organ. The registration should obviously reflect the solemnity and joy which attends the entering of the precincts of God. It should not reflect the theater or the concert hall. Keep it within dignified bounds.

The Choice and Presentation of the Voluntary

The voluntary, coming as it does almost immediately after the sermon, offers the congregation a time to meditate upon the truths just presented. It is essentially reflective in character. It may also serve to introduce the hymn which follows the prayers. The organist is safe in following the general rules laid down for the choice of a prelude.

In most churches the offerings are received during the playing of the voluntary. This circumstance creates two problems: in the first place, it tends to make the congregation feel that the voluntary is merely a cover for the sound of falling coins and that it serves only the purpose of entertaining more money out of reluctant pockets; in the second place, it usually determines the length of the voluntary. The organist must attempt through his selection of the voluntary and his careful playing of it to make the voluntary a meaningful liturgical part of the service. This can, of course, best be done by relating the music to a hymn in the service, preferably either the office hymn or the one to follow the prayers. Organists generally have made the mistake of using the time of the voluntary to play something pretty and entertaining, and to that end have too often chosen secular and romantic music. This practice introduces a false note into the service by attracting attention to the music instead of to the sermon and the hymns, and serves to destroy the unity of the service at a most crucial point. It is almost as if the organist were saying to the congregation, "Well, it's about over, and you can now re-enter a more congenial world. Don't take what you have heard too seriously."

The limitation on the length of the voluntary is not necessarily an evil thing. If, by agreement with the pastor and those who receive the offerings, it is made possible to vary the length of the voluntary slightly from Sunday to Sunday according to the music being played, this limitation becomes only a mechanical problem of signaling the end of the piece. There should be an agreement that the officiant will not step to the altar until the voluntary has been completed.

It is common and good practice to play the voluntary on a subdued registration. Quiet registration does indeed provide a setting suitable for meditation. There is no law we know of, however, which prevents an organist from using music which demands louder registration. Certainly

48

not all services give rise to identical meditative moods. There can and should here also be variety in the types of music and the fitting registrations.

The Choice and Presentation of the Postlude

The choice of postlude is conditioned by most of the same factors which determine the choice of prelude. The postlude is merely the other half of the frame. Generally, the postlude is a more joyful piece of music and freer in style and character. The postlude should reflect the dominant note of the service, and it will usually contain a note of joy to support the joy which worshipers feel upon having met God in the service. Except for the above specific comments, what has been said regarding the choice and the presentation of the prelude and the voluntary applies also to the postlude.

Source of Materials

It is not our purpose to write a music catalog. Many excellent music catalogs exist which need not be duplicated here, among them the catalog specifically designed for Lutheran organists by Concordia Publishing House. It may be in place, however, to indicate the most fruitful sources of materials for the purposes previously outlined. For preludes to chorales we turn to the period from 1550 to 1800, during which time the chorales of the Lutheran Church and the preludes based upon them were created. The preludes, postludes, fugues, fughettas, etc., which were written during this period were written for a functional use in the service. They are still today the finest organ music available, both from the purely musical standpoint and from the standpoint of suitability for worship. In difficulty they range from the simplest to the most difficult.

For preludes on hymns other than chorales one must necessarily look to more recent compositions. By no means all of the hymns found in the average hymnal have been used as material for organ pieces. There is a dearth of suitable material in this area. It is also true that much of the material which is available is of doubtful quality or worse. However, such composers as Willan, McKinley, Bingham, and Thiman have written hymn-tune preludes of real musical worth and suitability. The *Parish Organist,* recently edited by Heinrich Fleischer, is another evidence that worthwhile materials are once again being written.

In addition to hymn-tune and chorale preludes there are many fine "nonthematic" pieces which are eminently suited by their dignity for use in worship. Simple preludes, fugues, toccatas, and voluntaries exist in abundance. The works of Bach, Buxtehude, Pachelbel, and many, many others abound in excellent music of this type. In general and for most services, it is best to avoid the flashiest and longest compositions in this field and choose those which will best lend themselves to the support of the Word, the sermon, and the hymns.

Special Services

What has been said thus far has had reference primarily to the usual Sunday service. The principles are valid not only for those services, however, but also for certain special services which frequently give the organist trouble, such as weddings and funerals. Weddings and funerals are still services to God, and therefore the music has the same relationship to the service in these cases as it does in the ordinary Sunday worship. This is a point which is sometimes most difficult to explain to the families immediately involved in one of these types of service. Very often they look upon the service as a service to themselves, rather than to God. They remember a beautiful piece of music heard at another funeral or wedding, or perhaps over the radio, or in a well-remembered movie scene, and then tend to insist that this music must be played or sung. They are often totally unaware that the service must be directed toward God and not toward the bridal couple or the deceased.

Musicians, on the other hand, frequently overstep their bounds on the other extreme. They will often fight against certain pieces of music not because they are secular or have secular connotations, but because the music is inferior, purely on musical grounds. It is true that the musician should at all times make every effort to improve the quality of music heard in his church, but he must at all times also keep in mind that purely musical considerations place a bad third behind the dedication of the music to God, and the helpfulness of the music to man. It will help to keep one hard fact in mind: The only thing upon which the musician has a right to insist is that the words and the music used in worship be dedicated to the worship of God. In all other areas the musician is clearly in the role of a guide and teacher who by patient persuasion must gradually win his people to higher musical standards.

With respect to the wedding service, the musician has a right and duty to point out to those being married (and particularly also to the bride's mother) that the words of such songs as "I Love You Truly," and "Because" are not directed toward God and therefore cannot be used in a service of worship to God. The problem of the usual wedding marches is not quite so easily solved, however, since the connotation of these pieces for most people is that of a religious ceremony. The plea that these pieces have an operatic origin is weak on two counts: first, because origin never determines function absolutely, and second, because the origin of the music plays practically no part in the thinking of those who wish to have it used.

Obviously, these wedding marches, radically unchurchly in character, and rendered banal by overuse, are not good music for the service. How much more meaningful it would be to have the bride and the groom approach the altar to the tune of "Let Us Ever Walk with Jesus" or "Lord, We Come Before Thee Now" or a host of other hymns and hymn preludes which would really express the significance of the occasion! The writer has found that many couples are grateful for suggestions of this kind and are eager to make their weddings more meaningful spiritually. But let us remember to make it clear that our actions in this are advisory. Man-made laws are just as bad when the musician makes them as when the clergy makes them. And man-made laws are self-defeating.

In choosing suitable vocal and instrumental music for weddings it is not at all necessary to find something which has specific reference to weddings. Any religious music which has a joyful or prayerful character will be found to be suitable. In addition to the hymns mentioned above, pieces such as the following are frequently used and eminently suitable: "Jesu, Joy of Man's Desiring," "God, My Shepherd, Walks Beside Me," "The Song of Ruth." Many more can be found in good catalogs and in special publications of wedding music.

Also for funeral services the finest music will be found to be that which is based upon a fitting hymn or chorale. The abundance here is so overwhelming that it is no problem to find suitable selections. A suggestion regarding the character of funeral music may here be in place. It is, unfortunately, quite customary to use for funeral services the most sorrowful music available and to play it upon the most sentimental registration in the organ. This habit belies the essentially joyful character of the Christian funeral service. It is, of course, true that the death of a loved one is a saddening occasion even for Christians, and it is also true that a funeral reminds us all of the sobering fact of our personal mortality. And yet death for a Christian is actually a victory. The music heard from the organ should properly reflect Easter — not Good Friday. The organist can perform a great and necessary service to the family of the deceased by emphasizing the Christian's sure hope of eternal life in the music he chooses to play, and in the manner of playing.

CHAPTER 9

Special Problems and Techniques in Service Playing

WE now turn to some problems and techniques which could not easily be included in preceding chapters in which we have been dealing with the chief music of the service. Among these somewhat unclassifiable topics are the following:

Bridging
Modulation
Accompanying
Improvisation
Unifying the service

Bridging

By the term bridging we here refer to the process of leading easily from one part of the service to another, usually by means of organ music improvised at the time. When we hear of a service as having been played "smoothly," without uncomfortable hitches and halts, it is usually excellence in the art of bridging which is referred to. As in most things artistic, the least bridging is the best, otherwise the congregation loses interest in the trip for concern about the bridges.

Probably the most common point at which skill in bridging is essential is between the introduction of the hymn and its singing by the congregation. This particular point might, in fact, better be named a "leap" than a bridge. The practice (heard in some churches) of ending each introduction with a series of chords culminating in the dominant seventh chord is in very poor taste. So also is the scarcely less tasteless practice of opening the Swell box while holding the last chord to signal the beginning of the singing.

If the introduction is properly played, the congregation will hear the end of the introduction and does not need a special signal to begin singing. The problem is almost entirely a rhythmic one. During the playing of the introduction the organist must develop a strong feeling of the correct tempo. But this is not enough. It is necessary further to continue this tempo through the pause between the introduction and the singing.

Another spot at which bridging is necessary is between the prelude and the first hymn. We have probably all experienced the uncomfortable wait between the last note of the prelude and the first note of the hymn introduction in a service played by an unskillful organist. This uncomfortable pause can best be eliminated in the following manner. Immediately after the prelude there should be a slight pause signaling the end of the prelude. But immediately thereafter the organist should play a series of chords which will lead from the prelude to the key and rhythm of the first hymn. This will afford a smooth connection between the prelude and the first hymn and also serve to set the actual rhythm and tempo to be used in the introduction and playing of the hymn.

Bridging is necessary also between the Amen and the Introit in those instances where the Introit is sung by the choir. Here, since the congregation is not involved in the chanting of the Introit, a very quick method of modulation is desirable. In instances such as this, where a quick modulation is preferable, a good method is the following: After the last chord of the Amen, go immediately to the first chord of the modulation on a soft registration which is suitable to be used as background for the choir's chanting. Use the fewest number of chords possible and proceed to the first note of the Introit.

In some instances the congregation is asked to rise before singing a certain portion of the service. This occurs, for instance, between the Votum and the Offertory where a congregation does not rise for the Votum. Here it is necessary only to play the opening chord or motive on a medium registration and then to play the accompaniment on a fuller organ for the singing.

The organist is often faced with the necessity of improvising extended endings in special mechanical circumstances, such as the seating of latecomers, and instances when individuals must approach the altar for commissioning to certain offices in the church. Another example of this kind is to be found in those cases where the pastor proceeds to the lectern after having been at or before the altar. In all these cases it is advisable to pick up both the key and melodic material from music which has very recently been played in the service, or which in a few moments will be played, so that the bridging material is not extraneous to the materials heard in the immediate vicinity of the bridges.

There are other locations in the service where bridging is necessary, but the problems will be found to be identical with, or similar to, those enumerated. In general, the short bridges should be made by the quickest possible modulation, and the longer bridges should be made as thematic and as well related to other materials in the service as is possible.

Modulation

Modulation is obviously one of the most necessary elements in good bridging, because key changes are frequent and sometimes very abrupt. Any discussion of modulation must necessarily presuppose a rather thorough knowledge of elementary harmony. This we cannot supply here, but we may be able to point to certain techniques and methods of modulation which are indispensable to good service playing.

In those cases where an abrupt modulation is called for, as for instance between the Amen and the Introit, use the simplest and most direct method possible. It will be found easiest and most direct to go from the last chord of the preceding music directly to the Dominant 7th of the new key on the new registration and then to the tonic of the new key. It is good practice to use the V_7 in first inversion (third in the bass) since the third of the V_7 is also the leading tone of the new key and will provide a greater drive into the new key. Try to keep at least one tone common to the two chords for the sake of smoothness. See Examples 1A and 1B on page 55.

A more leisurely type of modulation which can be used when speed is not required and which is by far more satisfying musically is modulation by means of a common chord. Here it is necessary to recognize the classification of chords within a tonality.

Example 1a

Modulation

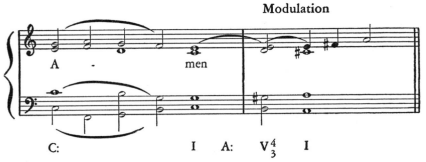

Introit follows in key of A major

Example 1b

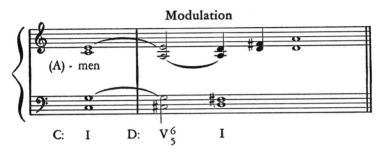

Introit follows in key of D major

Chord Classification

Tonic
Class 1: V and vii
Class 2: IV, ii, and I$^6_4$
Class 3: VI
Class 4: iii

This classification system means that the normal progression of harmony is from iii to VI to either IV, ii, or I$_4$, to V or vii to the tonic. Knowing this, we can proceed to find chords which are common to two keys which are involved in a modulation. For example, if we wish to proceed from the key of C to the key of D, we will first choose a chord which is common to both keys. We see immediately that the V chord in the key of C (gbd) is identical with the IV chord in the key of D. We would play the V chord in the key of C, mentally rename it the IV chord in the key of D, and then cadence in the key of D. Actually this would require only four chords. See Example 2 on page 56.

Example 2

C: I V = D:IV V₇ I

It is well to remember when searching for common chords that for all practical purposes in any improvisation, major and minor chords are absolutely interchangeable. If, for instance, you desire to modulate from the key of C to the key of E♭, you may consider the following chords as being identical for purposes of modulation.

Key of C	Key of E♭
I. ceg	VI. ce♭g
IV. f a c	II. f a♭ c
V. g b d	III. g b♭ d

Example 3

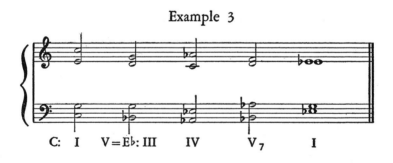

C: I V = E♭: III IV V₇ I

Several frequent modulations give considerable trouble and cannot be solved readily by any of the methods which have so far been mentioned. One of these is the modulation from a key to the key a half step below. This troublesome modulation can very satisfactorily be solved by proceeding from the I_6 chord with doubled third of the old key to the I_4^6 chord of the new key and then cadencing.

Example 4

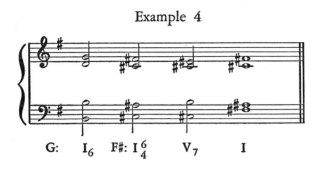

G: I_6 F♯: I_4^6 V_7 I

The reverse problem, modulating from a key to the key a half step above, can be solved by reversing this procedure.

Example 5

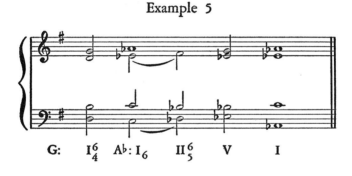

G: I_4^6 A♭: I_6 II_5^6 V   I

All longer modulations should preferably be made thematic. This is a skill which requires some practice but is extremely rewarding in terms of the smoothness and fittingness of the modulations. The thematic material will obviously be selected either from the music from which you are going, or from the music to which you are leading, or both. The organist begins in the key and character of the music which has just been completed, using a very short motive, which may be no longer than three notes, and then by means of the pivotal chord enters the key of the new music and introduces the beginning motive of that music. See Example 6 on page 58.

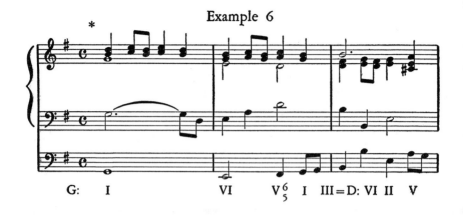

Example 6

G: I   VI   V $^6_5$ I   III = D: VI II   V

Hymn 2

To Thy tem-ple

etc.

I $_6$ VII $_6$ I   V $_7$ I

* Motive from Preludio in G — Joh. G. Walther

Several additional suggestions may be in place with regard to all modulations regardless of the harmonic technique employed.

1.   Spread the chords as widely as possible to avoid clumsiness. Do not be satisfied with having the bass note in the pedal and a cluster of notes in the right hand. Treat the modulations as much as possible in a vocal manner, being careful to spread the voices apart and to lead them as naturally as possible.

2.   Practice modulations. Modulation is a technique which depends upon familiarity with the materials of harmony and a few methods of procedure. Practice is imperative. Since the key of G is so often used in service playing, a good plan of practice would be to practice modulation to all keys from the key of G, and to practice modulating from all keys to the key of G.

Accompanying

Accompanying is not the least difficult of the arts which an organist needs to acquire. At its best it provides a firm but unobtrusive support for soloist or singers. The accompaniment must be neither ahead nor behind in tempo. If the accompaniment provides a significant addition to the music with a minimum of doubling of voice parts, it should be registered brightly and clearly, but always, of course, in such a way as not to cover the voices. The value of accompaniments which are merely exact repetitions of the vocal lines is largely psychological and should be dispensed with when possible.

Where the director of the choir is also the accompanist, it will be necessary for him to learn how to signal with his left hand while playing. This is again a skill which needs considerable practice. It requires not only that the director be able to signal with his left hand and play at the same time, but it requires also the ability so to rearrange the music that it can be adequately presented when played by right hand and pedal alone. It should not be necessary to continue beating time once the rhythm has been established and the choir has begun singing. It will, of course, be necessary to signal throughout the composition for further attacks, releases, and dynamic or tempo variations. See Example 7 on pages 60 and 61.

In accompanying solo songs, it is often necessary to rearrange the written accompaniment to make it suitable for the organ. The typical pianistic broken or repeated chord accompaniment sounds thin and inadequate on the organ, which requires a sustained form of writing. It is best to play the chord as a static chord and then to play separately whatever melodic material is present or can be improvised. Often it is advisable to use two manuals, one for the purely chordal material and one for the melodic material. See Examples 8A and 8B on pages 62 and 63.

Improvisation

In the widest sense, improvisation means any music played which has not been previously composed and written down. Bridging and modulation are included under this definition. In the narrower sense in which we here use it, it means the creation of larger pieces of music used as preludes, voluntaries, postludes, and music played during the distribution of Holy Communion. Unfortunately, this kind of improvisation is almost a lost art. Its loss has meant a loss of spontaneity and

(Continued on page 64)

Example 7

* **Written:**
Men's voices

* King of Glory, King of Peace, Eric Thiman. Novello & Co., Ltd., London. 1930

Example 7 continued

Played:

Example 8a

Written:

F. MENDELSSOHN

Andante con moto (♩ =72)

"If with all your

hearts ye tru-ly seek Me, ye shall ev - er sure · ly

find Me." Thus saith our God. "If with

Example 8b

Played:

inventiveness in service playing. The organist has come to feel that all music in the service must be previously selected and arduously practiced. The emphasis has come to be placed upon correct execution rather than upon the playing of music fitted in spirit to the spirit of the worship being conducted. There are many times when a piece which has been previously selected as fitting for a particular service does not seem, when one is actually in the midst of the service, to be fitting at all. The well-versed organist should here be able to improvise according to the spirit of the service as it has now become apparent to him. The result of a skillful improvisation in a situation of this kind will be an unmistakable gain in the unity of the service and in the transmission of a genuine spiritual experience. The technique of improvisation would be particularly valuable with respect to hymn tunes other than chorales on which little or nothing is available in print.

The reason why not more organists improvise is that they are afraid that they cannot. Their training and experience has all been in the direction of reproducing faithfully what has been written. Actually, improvisation can and should be considered simply speaking in music, and it should be natural and unforced. Organists need to learn to think in musical terms and to express thoughts in musical form.

There are really only two essentials beyond the ability to play the instrument which are needed in order also to be able to improvise. These are a knowledge of harmony and the ability to imagine music. With this basic equipment the following skills need to be developed.

1. A physical sense of the keyboard. One must be able to "think with one's fingers."

2. A sense of balance in musical structure. The ability to imagine music according to a formal structure, however simple.

3. A knowledge of style in composition and the ability to vary the style in improvisation.

Acceptable improvisation is, again, a technique which can be learned like any other technique, through directed practice. The following list of suggested exercises can improve improvisation technique immeasurably.

Exercise A. Take a book of folk songs or any other book of unaccompanied tunes. Choose a simple tune and play it. Sing it over without playing it. Then listen to it in your mind. Next play a bass with it. Next play it in three parts. Next transpose it to a number of other keys.

Exercise B. Imagine original tunes to a point of clarity where you will be able to go to the piano and play them with few or no errors. Use your own tunes as materials for the same exercises as suggested in example A.

Exercise C. Take a short theme and improvise in two parts imitatively; that is, try to make the second part an equal part with the first by the use of melodic material from the first part. Using the same technique, improvise in three and four parts.

Exercise D. Using as a model a simple chorale prelude from any standard collection of chorale preludes, improvise in the various styles one will find there on hymns found in your hymnbook.

Obviously this is not a complete course in improvisation, nor will the above exercises make of anyone a finished improviser. They will, however, give a person a start upon the road at the end of which he will find the thrilling ability to play as he feels the need to play.

In all improvising the following points should also be kept in mind.

1. Always play in rhythm.

2. Always be conscious of the harmonic direction. (Here consult the chord classification system previously noted, and also keep in mind the circle of fifths and the circle of fourths to keep key relationships within the proper harmonic framework.)

3. Always keep the texture clear. Be careful that the parts are spaced widely enough to be heard individually. Do not change from three to four or four to five parts within any one improvisation.

4. Always play completely without reference to notes.

Unifying the Service

Not all of the elements in a service are subject to the control of the musician. Among those parts of the service which the musician cannot control are the fixed parts of the liturgy, the sermon, and the choice of hymns. Some pastors do consult their organist on the choice of hymns, and this practice is to be commended. In most cases, however, the hymns are chosen by the pastor in order to fit the message of the Scripture readings and the sermon. The organist can and does control, however, all the set organ pieces and the choir selection. Here he must maintain and, if possible, enforce the unity set up in the propers, the sermon, and the hymns. The following suggestions will be found helpful in achieving unity in the service.

1. Ask the pastor to supply a list of hymns, text of sermon, and the main emphasis of the sermon for a longer period of time in advance.

2. Choose the organ and choir selections on the basis of this information plus a reading of the Scriptures appointed for each Sunday.

3. Unity is not uniformity, and it does not require that every piece of music in the service must be on the specific subject of the sermon. Not everything in the service needs to be precisely on the same topic. There should, however, be a logical relationship. It is possible to fill out a train of thought or to reflect an idea with a somewhat altered emphasis. For instance, it is not mandatory that the organ play and the congregation and choir both sing "A Mighty Fortress" on Reformation Day. Some other Reformation hymn could be sung by the choir, and the voluntary could be played on that hymn or on still another Reformation chorale. The unity achieved in any service should not be painfully obvious, but it must be there and it must be possible intuitively to feel it.

4. No matter how far previously you have selected the music for a particular service, it is nevertheless imperative that a few days before the service is to be held the organist once again go over all the elements of the service to make sure that no situations have changed.

5. Just before playing, go over again in your mind all the parts of the service so that even the mechanical bridgings are affected by the spirit of that particular service. Here it might very well be in place to mention that the organist should, if at all possible, reserve the period immediately before the service for quiet consideration of the duty he is about to perform. It is not good practice to rush breathlessly from a Sunday school class on to the organ bench. The excellent practice of having a brief choir rehearsal before the service affords the organist a real opportunity to get himself and his choristers into the proper frame of mind for the work which is to follow. This practice also serves to create understanding between the organist and the singers with particular reference to the service about to begin.

The Church Concert

The church concert is an ancient institution which is under severe sociological attack today. Professional and widely disseminated entertainment, available in the neighborhood movie theater or at the labor of turning a button on the radio or television set occupies large areas of the time which in previous generations and under different attitudes toward the church has been spent in the music or other activities of the church. Added to this is the greatly increased mobility of contemporary America through the automobile. Besides these sociological circumstances there is the fact that, by and large, church concerts of today are among the most conservative and reactionary of all concerts. The church is inherently conservative because its first aim is to pass on a tradition. But it is often conservative to the point of forgetting that it must also always face the future as well as the past. The American concert-going public is accustomed to hearing new works by new composers as a regular part of its musical diet. In the church, while the music lover finds musical sanctuary, he finds little or no musical adventure.

The church concert is eminently worth saving, however, because it represents the fact that church music may be enjoyed simply as music in addition to its enjoyment as an adjunct to worship. The church concert also emphasizes the obligation of the church to cultivate the whole man and to contribute something to the community in cultural areas of life as an outgrowth and an expression of a Christian view of life, which engages the total personality and the total society.

The church concert should be used by the musician to present great religious music of both the past and the present which may not have been written specifically for the service or which, because of length or other considerations, does not fit well into the service. It is necessary always to center even the church concert about a religious idea or a spiritual emphasis of some kind. This will, in fact, give the concert added force. Probably the greatest error which can be made is to permit the church concert to become self-conscious musically or to use the church concert as a propaganda platform for purely musical ideas. The church concert must finally and pre-eminently serve the Gospel.

CHAPTER 10

Organ Registration and Design

Registration

OUR previous references to registration have been specifically with regard to certain portions of the service and have necessarily been limited because of the wide variations found in organs. However, some general statement on organ registration may be helpful in choosing fitting registration for various types of organ pieces. It will first of all be helpful to recognize the various classifications of tone found in an organ. The two main divisions of organ tone are basic tone and "characteristic" tone.

BASIC ORGAN TONE

Masculine (open pipes, usually cylindrical in shape)

1. Principal (Diapason) (16', 8', 4', 2')
2. Octave (4', 2', 1') (Superoctave; Fifteenth)
3. Quint (Twelfth; 2⅔', 1⅓')
4. Mixtures (Fourniture, Scharff, Zimbel, Plein Jeu)

Feminine (open, covered, and partly covered)

1. Gedackts
   16' Subbass
   16' Lieblich Gedackt, 8' Quintadena
   16' Bourdon, 8' Stopped Diapason
   8' Gedackt, 8' or 4' Rohrfloete
   8' or 4' Koppelfloete
2. Flutes
   8' or 4' Gemshorn, 8' or 4' Rohrfloete, 4' Spitzfloete
   4' Harmonic Flute, 4' Hohlfloete
   2' Blockfloete, 2' Waldfloete, 2' Piccolo, 2' Flautino,
   2⅔' Nasat or Nazard, 1⅓' Larigot
   4' or 2' Nachthorn

Labial Pipes

> The string stops
> > Salicional (Voix Celeste)
> > Viola da Gamba (Viola Celeste)
> > and derivatives

Reed Pipes

1. Conical resonators
   Trumpet
   Oboe
   Fagott
   Posaune
   Clarion
   Schalmey

2. Cylindrical resonators
   Krummhorn
   Rohrschalmei
   Clarinet

3. Short-length resonators
   (less than ½-pitch length)
   All regals (Vox Humana)
   Rankett
   Sordun

Under basic organ tone we have included such stops as are historically indigenous to the organ only, and compared to which the reeds and strings are considered additives. Characteristic tone is usually used not in the basic organ ensemble but for added color and as an addition to, and foil for, the basic color of the organ. Pipes in this class tend not to blend easily with pipes of basic organ tone. They are constructed and voiced with a view toward producing a unique, singular tone that generally is sufficient unto itself and resists combination. Often these pipes imitate orchestral instruments either of the present or of more ancient times.

Stops can be combined on the organ in any of three ways. They may be used to achieve a plenum, a background, or a solo combination.

A. Plenum. Plenum registration is used when the entire music is to be played on one manual at a time, that is, when a solo-and-accompaniment situation is not desired. A plenum requires a minimum of two pitches, the higher one of which is from the masculine family of basic organ tone. The registration should be clear and bright to reveal the contrapuntal texture of such music. Even when playing homophonic music the combination should include stops of higher than 8′ pitch in order to avoid a heavy sound. The dynamic range possible is from mf to ff. Plenum registration is used for hymns, preludes, offertories, fugues, and both harmonic and contrapuntal textures. Examples of plena:

1. Gedackt, 8′
   Principal 4′
2. Principal 8′ and 4′
3. Quintadena 8′
   Rohrfloete 4′
   Principal 2′
4. Principal 8′ and 4′
   Mixture III or IV
5. Principal 8′ and 4′
   Rauschquinte II
6. Quintadena 16′
   Principal 8′
   Octave 4′
   Mixture III or IV

B. Background. As the name implies, this type of registration is used for the accompanying parts in solo and accompaniment pieces, and for accompanying soloists and small ensembles. The tone should be yielding, not aggressive, but also not dull. Depending upon the individual voicing, background registration may be of one or several stops, preferably of two pitches. One does not use stops from the masculine family for this type of registration. Examples of background registration:

1. Spitzfloete 8′ or Gemshorn 8′, each individually
2. Gedackt 8′ and Rohrfloete 4′
3. Rohrfloete 8′
   Spitzfloete 4′
4. Rohrfloete 8′
   Spitzfloete 4′
   Flautino 2′

The accompaniment in the typical solo-and-accompaniment chorale prelude should not be dynamically far from the solo. The background and solo should be differentiated primarily according to color, not according to volume.

C. Solo. Here are included the characteristic stops, such as solo reeds and the more characteristic string tones. It is not always necessary, however, to use the most characteristic tones available on the organ for a solo stop. Often a single flute or principal may be used as a solo instrument if the voicing happens to be good. One must also not overlook the possibility of using a 4' stop played an octave lower than written for either the solo or the accompaniment registration. The most interesting and varied solo tones can be achieved by combination. Particularly "skip-pitch" registration offers great possibilities. Examples of "skip-pitch" solo registration:

1. Gedackt 8'
   Piccolo 2'
2. Gedackt 8'
   Nazard 2⅔'
3. Gedackt 8'
   Nazard 2⅔'
   Tierce 1⅗'
4. Gedackt 8'
   Flute 4'
   Nazard 2⅔'
   Tierce 1⅗'

Probably the finest solo combination is the so-called "Cornet," which is a compound of the following pitches: 8', 4', 2⅔', 2', 1⅗'. On some organs these pitches are available on one draw knob or tablet. On others one must draw them separately. The sound of the "Cornet" is one of the finest, particularly for chorale preludes of the melismatic type. Many other examples of solo registration can be invented if you are fortunate enough to have an organ on which there are many mutations. A little experimentation will reveal an almost infinite number of possibilities in this field.

Frequently one finds these upper pitches present on unified organs. On unified organs these upper pitches are inescapably out of balance with the lower pitches because there is no real set of pipes corresponding to the stop. Instead, the manufacturer simply wires from the key to a pipe far above the normal pitch of the key. This means that the upper pitches cannot be colored to blend with the lower pitches and that particularly the off-pitch stops are out of tune. On such organs the result of unlimited use of these unified mutations is an unpleasant screaming and screeching, particularly when, in addition, the organist unwisely adds the 4' coupler. The suggestions made above are to be understood as referring to "straight organs," that is, organs in which there is a set of pipes for each stop.

While the use of the Swell pedal is not specifically a matter of registration, the position of the Swell pedals (whether open or closed) seriously affects the sound of the organ. The normal position of the Swell box is open. If the tone is too strong with the Swell box open, the first attempt at a remedy should be the removal of stops. The initial effect of the Swell shutter is to remove from the tone the most interesting parts of the tone, which are the upper partials. With these upper partials removed, the tones of an organ tend to sound dull, lifeless, and identical with one another. It is the number, selection, and relative intensity of these upper partials which enable organ builders to differentiate among stops of the same pitch. The real use of the Swell pedal is to provide delicate nuance in certain types of music. It is never, or almost never, its purpose to reduce the volume of the tone.

In many fine organs being built today, the Swell box is either eliminated entirely or confined to one division on large organs. Actually there is much less real need for the Swell box than is generally supposed. Most organ music will sound much better if nothing is placed between the pipes and the hearer.

The crescendo pedal also requires careful handling. The crescendo pedal should never have included in its range the 16' couplers, since these do nothing except muddy the tone of the organ by doubling everything an octave below. The crescendo pedal should be so adjusted as to provide a gradual increase from the softest to the most brilliant registration of which the organ is capable. It should not be used as a substitute for hand selection of stops by the organist. Its principal uses are to provide a quick change from soft to loud or vice versa, and to provide a gradual increase in volume, particularly at the conclusion of pieces in which a sustained growth in tone is required.

Suggested Organ Specifications

Following is a sample specification of a small organ which follows the best principles of organ design and will be found more than adequate for service playing. (In the main, this specification is the one used by Walter Holtkamp of Cleveland, Ohio, in the organ built by him for Concordia Teachers College, River Forest, in 1953.)

Pedal	Great	Swell
Subbass 16′	Copula 8′	(enclosed)
Gedackt 8′	Spitzfloete 4′	Quintadena 8′
Choralbass 4′	Principal 4′	Rohrfloete 4′
Great to Pedal	Cymbal II	Principal 2′
Swell to Pedal	Swell to Great	Sesquialtera II (2⅔′, 1⅗′)

1. Plenum Registrations

   Great

       a. Copula 8′ and Principal 4′

       b. Copula 8′ and Principal 4′ and Cymbal

   Swell

       8′ Quintadena and Rohrfloete 4′ and Principal 2′

   Pedal

       Subbass 16′, Gedackt 8′, and coupler

       Subbass 16′, Gedackt 8′, and Choralbass 4′

       Subbass 16′, Gedackt 8′, Choralbass 4′, and couplers

   Great and Swell coupled

       a. Copula 8′ and Principal 4′ and Principal 2′

       b. Copula 8′ and Principal 4′ and Principal 2′ and
          Cymbal II

2. Background Registrations

   Great

       Copula 8′ and Spitzfloete 4′

   Swell

       Quintadena 8′ and Rohrfloete 4′

   Pedal

       Gedackt 8′

       Subbass 16′, Gedackt 8′

3. Solo Registrations

   Great

       Copula 8′ and Principal 4′

       (a plenum registration which can be used as solo because
       of dynamic strength)

Swell

    Quintadena 8′ and Sesquialtera II
    Quintadena 8′ and Rohrfloete 4′ and Sesquialtera II
    Quintadena 8′ and Rohrfloete 4′ and Principal 2′ and
    Sesquialtera II

Pedal

    4′ Choralbass

The following sample specification, for a three-manual church organ, is by Paul Bunjes.

Great	Swell	Positive
16′ Quintade	8′ Gedackt	8′ Quintadena
8′ Prinzipal	8′ Gamba	4′ Spitzfloete
8′ Holzgedackt	4′ Prinzipal	2′ Italian Prinzipal
4′ Octave	4′ Rohrfloete	1⅓′ Klein-Nasat
2⅔′ Nasat	2′ Blockfloete	III Zimbel
2′ Octave	II Sesquialtera	8′ Krummhorn
IV Mixture	III Scharf	
	8′ Trompette	
	4′ Hautbois	
Pedal		
16′ Offenbass	8′ Quintade	8′ Posaune
16′ Subbass	4′ Choralbass	4′ Singend Cornet
16′ Quintade	III Rauschpfeife	2′ Singend Cornet
8′ Octave	16′ Posaune	

1. Plenum Registrations

Great

    a. 8′ Holzgedackt and 4′ Octave
    b. 8′ Holzgedackt, 4′ Octave, 2′ Octave
    c. 8′ Holzgedackt, 4′ Octave, 2′ Octave, IV Mixture
    d. Substitute 8′ Prinzipal for 8′ Holzgedackt in above
       registrations
    e. Full Great

Swell

    a. 8′ Gedackt, 4′ Prinzipal
    b. 8′ Gedackt, 4′ Prinzipal, III Scharf
    c. Substitute 8′ Gamba for 8′ Gedackt in above
       registrations
    d. Full Swell

Positive

    a.   8' Quintadena, 4' Spitzfloete, 2' Italian Principal

    b.   a and III Zimbel

    c.   Full Positive

Pedal

    a.   16' Subbass, 8' Octave

    b.   16' Subbass, 8' Octave, 4' Choralbass

    c.   b and III Rauschpfeife

    d.   Substitute 16' Offenbass for 16' Subbass in above registrations

    e.   Full Pedal

2. Background Registrations:

Great

    a.   8' Holzgedackt

    b.   16' Quintade, 8' Holzgedackt (play octave higher)

Swell

    a.   8' Gedackt

    b.   8' Gedackt, 4' Rohrfloete

    c.   b plus 2' Blockfloete

Positive

    a.   8' Quintadena

    b.   8' Quintadena, 4' Spitzfloete

Pedal

    a.   16' Quintade, 8' Quintade

    b.   16' Subbass, 8' Quintade

3. Solo Registrations:

Great

    a.   8' Prinzipal

    b.   8' Holzgedackt and 2⅔' Nasat

    c.   4' Octave

    d.   8' Prinzipal and 2⅔' Nasat (played octave higher)

Swell

    a.   8' Gamba, 4' Rohrfloete

    b.   8' Gedackt, 4' Rohrfloete, II Sesquialtera

    c.   8' Trompette or 4' Hautbois

    d.   8' Gamba, 2' Blockfloete

    e.   8' Gamba, II Sesquialtera

f.	8′ Gedackt, 4′ Prinzipal, II Sesquialtera (Archaic Cornet)
g.	Same as f plus 2′ Blockfloete (full Cornet)

Positive

a.	8′ Quintadena, 2′ Italian Principal
b.	8′ Quintadena, plus 1⅓′ Klein-Nasat
c.	8′ Quintadena, 2′ Italian Principal, 1⅓′ Klein-Nasat
d.	8′ Quintadena, plus III Zimbel
e.	4′ Spitzfloete plus 1⅓′ Klein-Nasat
f.	8′ Krummhorn

Pedal

a.	4′ Choralbass
b.	8′ Posaune
c.	8′ Posaune and 4′ Choralbass
d.	4′ or 2′ Singend Cornet
e.	4′ Choralbass and 2′ Singend Cornet

The above registrations are not intended to be exhaustive, but rather suggestive of the combinations possible in an organ of this size and composition. It must also be remembered that no organ can be built or played on paper. The sounds of the actual pipes finally determine registration.

CHAPTER 11

Practical Problems

Organization of the Choir

AMONG the problems which frequently rise to vex the choirmaster are some which have little or nothing to do with the actual performance of music. Many of these have to do with the organization of the choir. When one is dealing with many people and complex situations, it is important to establish routines which require little discussion and operate more or less automatically. The suggestions which follow are operating well in many choirs and will serve most groups, with alterations dictated by local situations.

Study the constitution of your congregation to see whether it says anything relating to the organization of the choir. It may make important stipulations regarding its relationship to the congregation. Some choirs have choir constitutions of their own, setting forth the routines by which the choir does its work. Most choirs will find that they are able to operate very well without a constitution, and, in fact, most choir constitutions are pretty well forgotten by the choirs themselves. It is advisable, however, to have officers in the choir who can serve as assistants to the choirmaster in many matters and particularly in those which are not primarily musical. It is in the best interest of a choir to turn over as many functions as feasible to the lay members of the choir. It will protect the choirmaster from falling into that ever-present human error of confusing himself with God in all matters which affect the organization. It will also serve to keep vitally interested members of the choir, who might not be challenged by an organization in which they are merely led like sheep. In most choirs it is found practical to have the following elected officers: president, vice-president, secretary, and treasurer. In addition, the following standing committees may be appointed and will be found eminently useful: library, robes, and social.

Finances

The music of the church should be the concern of the entire congregation. In many churches where the congregation does not contribute to the support of the music the choir descends to the level of a fund-raising organization. "As a man thinketh, so is he." If the members of the choir are constantly hard pressed to find sufficient money to finance their operations, they will begin to view their work in terms of the financial return which it may bring. Instead, then, of concentrating upon the purchase and performance of excellent church music, they may begin to think in terms of what kind of plays or operettas they may perform in order to raise money. For these reasons we oppose forcing the choir to finance its operations. The choir should receive a stated amount yearly, and it should dispense this money through its treasurer, subject to audit by the congregation. These moneys are, however, to be used only for such purposes as are directly related to providing and improving the music of the church. The little money needed for social purposes and gifts should come from dues and special projects of the choir.

Practice Room

The choice of a practice room is usually limited to rooms which were originally designed for other purposes, often a basement or a schoolroom. The average schoolroom is not a bad place for rehearsal, fortunately. The average basement, because of its low ceiling, is usually not a good place. Ideally, the practice room should be a high-ceilinged room with hard walls so the tone will be reflected to the singers. The room should be large enough to store robes and music, and it should be near enough to the choir loft in the church to provide quick and easy access. Its equipment should also include a good piano, a desk and a chair, and whatever else is necessary to make the room adequate as a workroom for the musical director. For choir seating, a good grade of folding chair is adequate.

Congregations which are planning a new church or school structure would do well to consider the possibility of providing a room for the musical activities of the church, which could also serve as a room for visual education and meetings of various committees in the church. Such a room earns its keep in utility and in the saving of wear and tear on the music and other equipment of the choir. Rooms of this sort have been provided in many churches which have been built recently and are proving themselves an excellent investment.

Choir Routine

Routine and discipline are important in any organization. Many choirs, indeed, fail of their full potential simply because no routine has been established and because discipline breaks down. Rehearsals should begin promptly in a relaxed but serious atmosphere. Begin with a consideration of Sunday's service. The director can refer to the Scripture readings and the sermon text and then go on to a singing of the hymns, the liturgical materials, and the anthem or motet. The choir should have a clear idea of the interrelationship of these materials so that they can intelligently participate in the service. After this part of the rehearsal has been concluded satisfactorily and while the singers are still fresh, go immediately into hard work on two or three selections which are in preparation for coming Sundays. At this point it is often found advisable to have a recess, particularly in the early part of the choir season, when the voices are still not in their best trim. After the recess devote the time to the reading of new materials and to a review once again of the liturgical materials and anthem for the coming Sunday service. This final brush-up of Sunday's materials should preferably be done in the choir loft in church. Throughout all the rehearsal aim for a religious and a singing experience for every one of the choristers. Don't lecture, but also don't fail to point out the significance of what you are asking the singers to do.

A definite routine should also be established for the choir on Sunday morning. The choir should be robed and in the rehearsal room ten or fifteen minutes before the service is to begin. During this time the choir should once again sing through all the materials to be used in the service. This is of the greatest importance. No choir should ever go into the service without having "warmed up." No matter how well the choir may know its music for the service, the first time that it sings it through is inevitably practice, and no choir has the right to practice in a service of worship. This is a matter of such importance that if there are mechanical hindrances to providing such a warm-up opportunity, they should be eliminated at all costs. After the service has been completed, the individual member should be responsible for putting away his books and robe. The librarian and the robe custodian will, of course, superintend this part of the operation and establish the suitable routine.

Care of Music

The librarian and his assistants are in charge of the music owned by the choir and of the filing and record system which operates to make the music readily usable and available. A simple but effective system is to file all anthems in envelope folders open at the top in a legal-sized drawer filing cabinet. As each new anthem is bought, give it its accession number. This means that if the anthem which you have bought is the 55th anthem in the choir's possession, the accession number printed on every copy of the anthem and on the envelope is number 55. Fill out a card for each anthem, showing its accession number, and file these cards alphabetically by the first word of the anthem's title. If you wish, you can have another file card filed separately according to the season of the church year in which the anthem can best be used.

Each member should have a folder numbered the same as his hymnbook and robe, if possible. Before each rehearsal the new music should be laid out on a table where it can be picked up together with the hymnbook and the liturgical books. After each Sunday's service the anthem which was sung can be returned to the table and placed back in its envelope by the librarian.

A chronological record of the choir's activities will be found to be of inestimable value to the director in planning future programs. This record can be kept in a large ledger and should note what has been sung at each service. In addition to this, the date on which a particular anthem is sung should be entered on the file card or cards for that anthem. Both of these records will prevent the choirmaster from repeating an anthem too often and will also help him to notice certain worthwhile pieces which might very well be repeated.

This system will work without any effort by the director once it has been put into operation. It provides a valuable musical record of the choir, showing its growth from year to year.

Choir Demeanor — Robing

Choir members must periodically be reminded that they serve a clerical function. Their musical services are not those of the concert choir or any other secular organization. Their primary concern is worship, not only for themselves, but also for all those who hear them. They should show by their demeanor both in and out of the choir loft that they understand this. This consideration applies, of course, to their total life, but even such minor irritating habits as talking, gum-chewing, and fidgeting in the choir loft are out of place on the same grounds.

Robing will be found to be helpful in achieving fitting behavior on the part of choir members because it hides many of the personal characteristics of the individual and emphasizes the common function of all. There is nothing quite so disturbing to worship as when people in the congregation note and perhaps discuss the clothing worn by the individual choir members. When the secular attire of the singers is covered with a robe which expresses their function in the service, such comment is impossible. The function of the choir can, we feel, be best expressed if the robe is composed of a black cassock and a white surplice. The black cassock is meant to symbolize the natural sinfulness of an officiant in worship, and the white surplice covering it is meant to symbolize the righteousness of Christ, which, like a white robe, covers all our sins. Ornaments, such as earrings and necklaces, which are visible outside of the robe should be removed.

Robes are expensive, and, unless the choir is very handsomely subsidized by the congregation, the robes cannot be expected to come out of the choir treasury but should rather be purchased by the congregation. The cleaning and repair of robes is best made the responsibility of the individual singer. The robe custodian should assign and fit the robes and report on the necessity for care or replacement.

Care of the Organ

In most congregations the organist is placed in charge of the organ, and it is therefore his responsibility to see to it that it is in playable shape mechanically and tonally. The best method is to have a service contract with a reputable organ service man and to report to him whenever work needs to be done. Minor tuning of individual notes, which sometimes go out of tune, can and should be done by the organist. A word of caution. Don't tune the organ too often. It must be expected that the organ will not always be in perfect tune because of frequent temperature changes in the American climate. This is particularly true during the winter months in churches which remain unheated except on Sundays. In most situations it will be found sufficient to have a general tuning only in late fall and late spring or early summer.

Choice of Organ

The best insurance a church can have that it will get an organ to suit its needs is the reputation of the builder whom it chooses to provide the organ. It is of the utmost importance to choose a reputable and financially responsible builder, whose previous work you have heard and liked and who gives evidence of understanding the function which the organ is asked to perform in your particular situation. If you are planning a new organ for a new church, be sure to have the architect consult the organ builder for space requirements and for treatment of the walls,

81

ceiling, and floor. Many tragedies have occurred because architects have left insufficient space for the organ, with the result that an organ of inadequate size has had to be installed or an organ of adequate size has had to be bottled up in a space which does not permit it to speak into the church. Other tragedies have resulted when the walls, ceiling, and roof of a church have been so deadened by sound-absorbing materials that the finest organ in the world would sound dull and inadequate.

An organ consultant, hired by the congregation for the purpose of advising the congregation on technical matters, and serving as its agent in dealing with the builder, will frequently be found to be a good investment. He can help the organist and the church committee in developing a good design and choosing the best builder for the particular design which has been found to meet the needs. The organ consultant can be particularly helpful when a congregation is enlarging or redesigning an organ. Unless the organist himself is well versed in all the many technicalities of organ building, or unless the builder is particularly adept at rebuilding (not all are or are even expected to be), it is best to secure competent advice.

CHAPTER 12

The Human Problems

THE Church of Christ on earth is a divine institution. It is the Body of Christ. Christ, however, willingly put it into the hands of men until the dawn of eternity. When He did this, He knew full well that men are fallible, subject to whims, prejudices, and errors of all kinds. The most consecrated, able, and sincere Christian is still a sinner. Man sees even Christ and His Word through fallible human eyes, and it is this faulty seeing which gives rise to divergence in doctrine and practice.

What is true on the universal scale in the Church is true also within a church body and within a local congregation. The general principle applies also in the specific case of music: Not all will agree on a given musical course; rather, they will differ both as to materials and methods. The problem of somehow coming to grips with these divergent viewpoints and resolving them into a course of action which will benefit the Church is a very real one and often determines the success or failure of a musician and the musical life of a congregation. The first thing to remember is that a particular kind of music or a particular procedure in the conduct of the Church's music has never been commanded by God. No one can speak on purely musical matters and claim to speak with the voice of God. The second thing to remember is that music in the congregation is not autonomous. Music is part of the total life of the congregation. There must be interaction with all the rest of the life in the congregation, each both nourishing and reflecting the other with the goal in view of a full recognition and enjoyment of the love of God in Christ. To fit a musical program to the life of a congregation requires that one know the people — their strengths, weaknesses, and potentialities, and then fit the music to the needs as well as one knows how.

In order to accomplish this, one must establish and maintain good working relations with the congregation as a whole and with their representatives. Music is not the private preserve of the musician. If the musician is to make a contribution, he must make it in terms of the understanding of his purposes by at least a majority of the people. His immediate contact with the people will be through various individuals and groups with whom he comes into frequent contact by reason of his work. It will be helpful at this point to discuss their areas of activity.

The Pastor

The pastor is the shepherd of the whole flock, placed in that position by God through the voice of the congregation. He is ultimately responsible to God for the spiritual life of the congregation in so far as he can, by his own acts and the acts of those placed under him by the congregation, affect it. He is also, in practice, the chief officer of the congregation in most cases. Leadership is expected to come primarily from him. Negatively stated, it is extremely difficult, if not impossible, to have a worthwhile musical program if the pastor is antagonistic, or lukewarm, or if he consistently and publicly expresses musical opinions contrary to those of the musical director. Positively stated, the musical life in a congregation will flourish if the pastor actively supports the musician.

The pastor must feel free to discuss the musical needs of the people as he sees them from the vantage point of the man who knows or should know best what the congregation needs spiritually. Unless the pastor is himself the musical director, however, he must not expect that his every whim will become law. The Law of God is still the law of love, and the method of the Gospel is persuasion, not compulsion. The pastor must recognize that the musical area has been specifically delegated by the congregation, not to him, but to the musician, and he must refrain from dictatorial words and acts.

The Musician

The musician has accepted responsibility for the conduct of music in a congregation. To that end he should equip himself spiritually and technically to the best of his ability. He should seek to come to an understanding of the pastor's point of view and to co-operate with him to the fullest extent possible. If he disagrees, he must have reasons for his position which go beyond the childish "I like it better my way." He should seek to be well versed in matters of church music and to develop a consistent philosophy with regard to the practice of church music. He must be willing to listen to suggestions and criticisms and to incorporate into his practice such things as are good. He must be

84

considerate of the needs and tastes of those whom he serves, but always mindful of his obligation to raise the level of both the spiritual and the musical understanding of his people. He must consider his co-workers in the church, and particularly the choir, as gifts of God which make it possible for him to do an acceptable service.

It is the responsibility of the musician to choose the music to be sung and played, to teach it, and to conduct its performance. No musician can accept responsibility for the music of the church if part or all of these functions are taken over by someone else. This is a responsibility which is just as clear as the pastor's responsibility to choose his text, write the sermon, and deliver it.

The Choir

The musician's most immediate and regular contact with the people of the church is through the choir. Choir members, taken as they are from many homes in the congregation, will reflect a good cross section of the spiritual and the musical level of the people. The wise musician will study their reactions to the music he chooses and encourage them to talk about their feelings with regard to it.

Choir members on their part can help by following directions as conscientiously as possible, by seeking to improve themselves as singers, and by seeking to interpret the musical program to the congregation as a whole. Choir members learn more about music than the average congregation member. They should share their increased knowledge and understanding with others to the benefit of the entire congregation.

Choir members will also do well to keep in mind that the direction of a choir under the manifold difficulties which are present in the church and in society today is an extremely difficult and often nerve-racking task. One of the chief blessings for which all choirmasters pray is that they may have choirs composed of people who are loyal to Christ, to the church, and to the organizations which they serve. Congregations will do well to remember that real loyalty to a choir requires that the members spend more time in this activity than is expected of the participants in almost any other volunteer activity in the church. Loyal choir members are certainly worthy of high regard in the estimation of their fellow congregation members.

The Music Committee

In some congregations a Music Committee has been established in order to effect liaison between the musician and other responsible boards in the congregation. If the congregation has delegated direction of music to the musician, then the Music Committee should not function in this area. Specifically, it should not choose the music or set itself up as judge of the director's professional acts. A fitting parallel is found here in the experience of many professional and amateur athletic teams. Where an owner or a board has hired a manager or coach for a team, it is recognized ethical procedure to give the manager full responsibility and full authority over the activities of the team. Where interference from the "front office" takes place, the success of the team, the career of the manager, and the profits of the owners all suffer most grievously. Generally speaking, if the music of the church is bad, the church needs a new musical director. Music Committees do not, and indeed cannot, produce music.

A Music Committee, can, however, make a worthwhile contribution. If the membership of the committee is made up of several members of the choir plus several members of the church council, it can serve to co-ordinate the musical with other activities of the congregation. It can inform the director of the success or failure of his program or parts of it. It can be helpful in suggesting new approaches and activities. It can be helpful in supplying new members for the choir. It can serve to acquaint the congregation with the needs of the musical program.

It is advisable to have at least one meeting a year with the Music Committee, or similar group, to review the preceding year's work and to present the plans for the new year for discussion and possible amendment or addition.

Other Colleagues

In most Lutheran congregations there are colleagues of the musician other than the pastor. Among these are other teachers in the school, assistant pastors, and educational directors. These can and should provide a consistent and powerful support for the musician. This is especially true of the teachers of the school. They can help immeasurably in providing a consistency and uniformity of direction in the music life of the church by asking and accepting musical advice from the music director of the church. They should seek to co-operate with him, for instance, in the establishment of a school choir, in the selection of hymns which the children of the school ought to learn, and by speaking favorably of the work which is done by the music director.

The musician will do well to have frequent informal meetings and discussions with the pastor and other colleagues. If he does not himself isolate music from the thoughts and life of his co-workers, it will not become isolated.

The human problems which the director faces are often determining as to the success or failure of his work in a given congregation. The musician cannot, of course, control all the elements in this problem, and it is true that some musicians have failed in this area because of the intransigence of others in the situation. If all those who are involved in the musical life of the church will remember that the final answer is to God, that God who sees the secrets of our motives will finally judge, most difficulties will vanish, and all difficulties will at least ameliorate. Most differences of opinion will revolve about the question of musical tastes. All parties to this dispute must remember that in the church we forget taste and emphasize worship; we forget music and think of God.

CHAPTER 13

A Lutheran Point of View

WHILE it is hoped that much found in these pages will be helpful to church musicians generally of whatever denomination, it is true that the book is written from a Lutheran point of view, because the author is a Lutheran and his direct experiences have been within the Lutheran Church. It is obviously important for a Lutheran to understand this point of view. What may not be so obvious is that the Lutheran point of view in music has considerable relevance generally in the field of church music.

In the first place, Luther, who first set the course of Lutheran music, retained much of the attitude and most of the forms in liturgy and music of the Medieval Church. Lutheran music, therefore, has its roots planted deep in historical tradition, as we have indicated earlier in these pages. In the second place, Lutheran music is the first Protestant music and shares the basic characteristics of all Protestant music, although later Protestant developments outside the Lutheran Church have departed in certain respects from Lutheran tradition.

To discover what is Lutheran will require that we seek to identify at which point or points Luther departed from the pre-existing medieval tradition and at which point or points the later Protestant developments have broken with Lutheran tradition.

The first approach to this problem must be theological, since theological considerations underlie the liturgical and musical differences. The theological discussion contained in the first section of this chapter is based upon a brilliant essay titled "Form and Tradition in Worship," by Dr. Jaroslav Pelikan of the University of Chicago.[10]

This essay gives clear expression to the underlying theological differences which have resulted in differing liturgical and musical attitudes in the Roman Catholic, Lutheran, and Protestant Churches. Dr. Pelikan points out that the Roman Catholic Church maintains a sense of historical continuity which Protestantism tends to repudiate.

[10] *First Liturgical Institute, Valparaiso University* (Valparaiso, Ind.: Valparaiso University Press, 1950), pp. 11—27.

Within the Roman Catholic Church there is a reverence for historical forms produced by the life of the Church because these forms are the product of the operation of the Church in history. In doctrinal as well as in liturgical matters, attitudes and forms acquire a holiness because of their origin in the Church and because of long use. An excellent example of this in the doctrinal field is, of course, the recent proclamation of the doctrine of the assumption of the Virgin Mary. Here is a doctrine not found in Scripture but proclaimed by the Roman Church because it has long been associated with that Church.

The Protestant Church, other than Lutheran, takes an attitude sharply opposed to this in both doctrine and practice. The Protestant Churches point out that God stands beyond history and the forms which history produces. Protestants generally are suspicious of the historical, because the Church has erred so often in history. Many Protestants consider the symbols of the past actually dangerous, because, along with their values, the contemporary Church is obliged to take also the errors from which no human product is ever completely free. Protestants generally also point out that no new direction can be taken in either doctrine or practice unless that direction is clearly outlined in Scripture. The doctrine of the assumption of the Virgin Mary is repudiated by Protestantism for this reason.

Associated with this feeling is a suspicion of intermediaries between the individual and God. Protestantism views the relationship between God and man as being an intensely personal and immediate one. For this reason it is inclined to remove even liturgical forms because of the human tendency to place faith in the mere act of going through a remembered formal procedure rather than in God. These attitudes have led many Protestant Churches to a denial of the historical element in the faith and life of the Church. It is for these reasons that many Protestant Churches are non-liturgical.

The Lutheran Church occupies a middle position with regard to doctrine and practice in these matters. Like the Roman Catholic Church, it accepts the historical and takes it seriously. But, unlike the Roman Catholic Church, it does not consider the product of history or of long use as being infallible and equal with God's own revelation. Like the Protestant Churches the Lutheran emphasizes individual participation and response, and immediacy of contact with God. But, unlike the Protestant Churches, it is unwilling to discard the products of the faith and life of the Church in times past. The Lutheran Church recognizes that the historical Church is not infallible any more than the contemporary Church is. But it also recognizes that the historical Church has been a repository of God's gifts in the past, gifts which were intended not only for the believers in their own time but for all time.

For these reasons the Lutheran Church is ecumenical in worship. There is found within the Lutheran Church a deep regard for forms, but no fixation upon particular forms. By definition, Luther's work was a reformation of the old Church, a cleansing within the historical framework; it was not an attempt to establish a new Church. The Lutheran Reformation was aimed not at the Church but against abuses which had germinated within the Church. Luther pointed out that the allegiance of Christian people had been subtly shifted from faith in God through Christ to faith in God through the saints, the clergy, and tradition. God had been veiled by means of intermediaries; Luther tore away the veil and reaffirmed the immediacy of contact with God.

So also in the musical and liturgical field. Luther did not create a new liturgy; rather he purified the old. He retained the outline and most of the parts of the Mass. He retained the music, chanting, vestments, and practically all the ancient practices of the Church. He did act, however, to remove language and musical barriers where these were an impediment to the worship of the individual Christian. To this end he encouraged the creation of German hymns, sometimes by re-forming ancient chants in metrical form, sometimes by setting Christian lyrics to music that was rather like folk songs.

In contrast to this, some of the Protestant groups abandoned all historical forms, removed the organs from the churches, wrecked the statuary, and constructed bare meeting houses in place of the great historical churches of the past. This attitude is inimical to both historical and contemporary human expression in the area of religion and worship.

This, then, is "Lutheran" in music and worship: To love, respect, and use the gifts which God has given His Church in times past; to discard forms when they breathe a spirit contrary to Scripture; to create new forms when the need arises. Lutheranism occupies a middle position which is able to make the best of two worlds — old and new. Lutheranism at its best is neither tradition-bound nor immaturely contemptuous of the past.

Historically, it is no accident that the Lutheran Church has produced the greatest Protestant music. The chorale was a new form. It was often used in a traditional manner (i. e., as part of the liturgy), and it was often based on an old text and old music. But it was a new form which met a need which is basic in the Lutheran view of the Church. It implicitly expressed the fact that all believers are priests in the eyes of God and can approach God directly. With the chorale as material, Lutheran composers constructed a literature which is unequaled in the history of Protestant music and, in fact, is the finest and fullest expression of the Christian faith in music.

And Now

For some years past American Lutherans have been much concerned about the question: "What is really Lutheran?" This question has been applied to theology, practice, music, liturgy, ceremonial, and a host of other related topics. Many answers have come, some tentatively and some with more assurance. It is to be doubted that there will at any time be a single unequivocal answer to this question in any field, since Lutheranism is as wide and as various as Christianity itself. Any attempt to narrow Lutheranism to a set of pat definitions will inevitably omit some part of the truth. Nevertheless, such questioning and answering is salutary, since it gives us clues to the approaches which may be found fruitful if applied to our contemporary problem.

With respect to music and liturgy our problem today seems to be the old and recurring one of the existence of a gap between those who worship and those who lead in worship. This gap is easily recognizable by anyone involved in leading worship, and its causes are not obscure. The Church today exists, as it were, as a cultural vestige. The society which surrounds it is completely secular. A world which worships money and power will inevitably find the *Te Deum Laudamus* curiously out of place.

There have been generally three answers to the existence of this gap attempted by the Church. One has been simply to continue operating as though no problem existed. This approach obviously offers no hope for a solution.

The second has been to eliminate as much as possible those forms which are not understood by the people and which are felt to be irrelevant. Note however, that in the example of the *Te Deum* above it is not the form as such which is not understood; it is the faith. Modern American society does not reject the form so much as it rejects God. It fails to see the relevance of individual forms because it does not recognize the worth of God. The elimination of traditional forms in and by itself will never solve the problem, because it removes only a surface aspect of a far deeper disease. In the attempt to combat secularism this solution succumbs to it.

91

The third generally suggested solution is a rather surprising one. It is argued that in order to make worship more meaningful it is necessary to resurrect and reintroduce ancient forms which are no longer in use. To this end there has been a strong movement to recreate the forms and practices which Luther himself advocated and used. Such a policy has two unfortunate consequences. In the first place, it tends to drive the Church further in upon itself and to emphasize still more its vestigial nature in the American cultural milieu. A consistent application of this philosophy will make of the Church a cult. In the second place, this solution evades the issue much as do the first two. The issue is not the forms, it is the faith. The resurrection of old forms in and by itself will not revive the faith because it revives only a surface aspect of something which is far deeper. In the attempt to combat secularism this solution avoids it.

The difficulty with these approaches is twofold. First, they do not attack the main problem. Second, they are at best only partial solutions even in the area where they apply.

The main problem to be solved, as previously stated, is the question of Christian faith. It is axiomatic that musical and liturgical forms are expressions. They are no more and no less than that: expressions of the faith. When, therefore, we attempt to solve musical or liturgical problems *on the basis of music and liturgy,* we are doomed to failure. It simply cannot be done. The problem must be attacked at its source, which is the faith. Viewed from the standpoint of worship, it is merely an idle exercise in musicology, for instance, to ask a contemporary choir to sing Bach's "Christ lag in Todesbanden," unless the singers understand what Easter means in their own lives. It can be stated as a fact that we may expect no real musical and liturgical revival in the hearts and minds of American Christians until there has been a revival of a deep and understanding faith. All attempts to improve music and liturgy on any other basis are idle, wasteful, and worse than useless. Here lies the fundamental weakness of the *a cappella* movement in the Church. The *a cappella* movement fastens its attention on one little segment of choral music, and from that moment on, its entire aim is to achieve a musical perfection in this restricted field. Predictably, it has become divorced from the life of the Church and has degenerated into a cult interested primarily in sound effects for their own sakes. While popular, the *a cappella* movement offers little or no hope for a regenerated musical life in the Church, since it is primarily music-centered rather than God-centered.

Secondly, the solutions under consideration are partial even in their own proper domain. Certainly we cannot solve our problem simply by eliminating the use of traditional forms; nor can we solve it simply by increasing the use of liturgical forms. If we become completely contemporary, we cut off our roots; if we become completely traditional, we clip the new flowers.

It is probably true that no historical tradition is ever completely applicable to a new set of circumstances. And yet the approach to the problem as it posed itself in the sixteenth century will certainly give us an important pattern to consider. In applying this approach it is important that we avoid confusing the approach with its sixteenth-century products. It is superficial to assert, as some have done, that, since Luther's efforts at solution led to the chorale, our solution lies simply in the chorale. Our solution may lead us to something entirely different but no less important for the problem at hand.

Luther's approach in liturgy was largely practical. He began with a keen sense of the value of the historical Church and its products, and he was unwilling to eliminate anything which was beautiful, true, and of value in worship. He did not wish to give his followers merely a personalized approach to God, but rather he wished to retain in public worship the sense of continuity which traditional music and liturgy so helpfully emphasizes. Consequently he eliminated nothing which was Scripturally correct. But he was not afraid to alter the tradition and to add to it. As we have noted earlier, he took parts of the liturgy and put them into hymn form to meet the need of encouraging people to worship more naturally and directly. He changed the language of the liturgy for the same reason. He began the creation of a whole new body of Christian song so that people could worship as real participants and not as spectators only.

This is the clue. Throw nothing valuable away, but at the same time, look forward, not back. To throw away ancient and beautiful liturgical forms and chorales, as some have done, is criminal. To teach the Church of Christ that it must forever worship only as it has worshiped in the past is equally so.

Practically speaking, what does this approach require of the twentieth-century leader in worship? It implies first of all that the first task of the musician, no less than that of the pastor or teacher, is to teach the Word. To teach the beauty of the liturgy or of the chorale without first and always teaching the Word is to build a house upon sand. On the basis of a strong and meaningful faith rooted in the Bible, it is possible to show that the beautiful liturgical forms and chorales bequeathed to us by the historical Church are pertinent to the faith and problems of today, because these forms speak a timeless language of a faith in an unchanging Christ. On the basis of this faith we must continue to inculcate the beautiful and meaningful traditions of Christianity. We must teach them in and out of season by showing how justly and beautifully they reflect the faith; by showing how the spiritual life of the church and the individual is nurtured and deepened by them; how they contribute to the fellowship of all the saints in Christ regardless of time.

At the same time those concerned with worship must be sensitive to the spiritual longings of man caught in the cataclysm of this time, a time of world upheaval, a time when man cries not for music, or liturgy, or even bread, but for some solid ground on which to stand as he faces the inevitable end — some faith, some sense of salvation beyond the apparent doom. When, in our time or later, men arise who feel this need, then will come the new music and the new liturgy without which the Church will remain artistically a miserable cult, forever picking over dry bones and feeding upon itself.

May God in His mercy grant the Church today the wisdom and the sensitivity to accomplish what the Church in time past has done: to bring to a bleeding world the mercy and triumph of the living Christ.

Index

Accompanying, 59

Ambrose, St., hymn writer, 9

Anthem, its characteristics, 17; composers, 17; function of in service, 38; style in presentation of, 42-43; verse anthems, 18

Antiphon, introit, 14

Background registration, 69, 70, 73, 75; use of, 70

Bernard of Clairvaux, hymn writer, 9

Bingham, Seth, composer, 49

Bridging, 52-54; definition of, 52

Cantate Domino, introit Fourth Sunday after Easter, 13

Cantillation, 12

Cantor, 16, 18

Cantus firmus, 17

Care of music, 79-80

Chant, liturgical, 12, 14; style in presentation of, 41

Choir, demeanor, robing, 80-81; finances, 78; organization of, 77-81; placement of, 43-44; practice room, 78; routines, 77, 79; warm-up, 79

Choir music; *see* Vocal music

Choirmaster, preparation of, 38

Choral song, purpose of, 15

Chorale, definition of, 16; liturgical use, 16-17; musical expression of the Reformation, 16; playing of, 30-36; style in presentation of, 41

Chorale motet; *see* Motet

Chorale preludes, 23

Chord classification, 55

Church music, didactic purpose, 8; difference between church music and secular music, 8; function of, 8; practical purpose, 8

Concert, church, 66-67

Congregational song; *see* Hymnody

"Cornet" registration, 71

Crescendo pedal, use of, 72

Examination packages, 40

Fleischer, Heinrich, 49

Funerals, choice of music for, 50-51

Gradual, 13

Gregory, St., 12

Hilary, hymn writer, 9

Hydraulis, 23

Hymn playing, artistic considerations, 31; introducing the hymn, 31-34; registration for accompanying congregation, 34-35; rules for, 30-31; special devices, 35-36; special problems, 36; technique of, 30-36

Hymnody, characteristics of, 14-15; Greek, 8; Latin, 9

Hymns, didactic value of, 9

Improvisation, suggestions for, 59-65

Instrumental music in worship, 20-25

Instruments, in worship at Bach's time, 21; in worship at time of Reformation, 20-21; in worship of Old Testament, 20; use of in worship, 21-22

Introit, Fourth Sunday after Easter, 13

Di Lasso; *see* Motet

Liturgical music, chanting of Introit and Gradual, 37-38

Liturgical song, 12

Liturgy, definition of, 26; outline of, 26-27; playing the music of, 26-29; rules for playing, 27-29

Luther, essay "Concerning Music," 11; high estimate of art of music, 9, 10, 11; interest in hymnody, 9; on worship, 1; views on art, 11; views on church music, 88-90; views on liturgy, 26, 90

Lutheran point of view, in church music, 88-94

Mass, 26

McKinley, Carl, composer, 49

Modulation, 54-58; thematic, 57-58

95